Singapore

HERITAGE FOOD

SINGAPORE HERITAGE FOOD

Sylvia Tan

Food photography by Ken Cheong

◊LANDM△RK◊BOOKS◊

PREFACE

A true Singaporean, it is said, will talk about his next meal while eating — and why not, our food is a lovely melding of at least four different cuisines: Chinese Malay, Indian and European. Instead of a clash of cultures, we have a unique culinary heritage that boasts well-loved and memorable dishes such as a chicken curry that is unlike any country's; a coconut noodle, laksa, that has found fans as far away as Australia and England; Singaporean inventions such as Ponggol chilli crab; a Chinese New Year raw fish salad and a truly multiracial mee goreng cooked up by an Indian stall holder using Chinese noodles, Western sauces and loved by all races.

Diverse cultures aside, there have been other influences at work throughout our history that have created the food of modern Singapore. In this tentative account of Singapore's food history, I have attempted to identify a few of them. The entry into this region of the various colonising powers: the Portuguese, the Dutch and the British, brought their individual food preferences and ingredients. The rise of regional trade resulted in the intermingling of food cultures, in particular influences from the Indonesian islands. The high profile of American culture after World War II brought Singaporeans their first taste of soda fountain food. There were the particular contributions from Hainanese and Cantonese cooks and intermarriage and travel have definitely developed our taste buds. More recently, increased educational and work opportunities for women saw the growth of demand for our very own convenience foods, a demand which has been met ably by Singapore food manufacturers.

What we have now is a culinary language and heritage that is unique, but which we probably take for granted, even if our after-dinner conversations centre on food.

It has been difficult to put together even this short account of our food history; it is a subject that has been little documented and sadly neglected by social historians. Old cookbooks, musty newspapers and most invaluable of all, informal chats and interviews with senior citizens who still remember old forgotten tastes, have proven invaluable.

I have attempted to describe not only the factors and influences at work in the food of Singapore, but also to list the dishes — and their recipes — that have come about. While I have tried to identify by research the influences found in the dishes we enjoy, some conclusions are no more than what I have deduced. Still, I hope that this book will provide a starting point for others similarly interested in the food we eat and how it came about to investigate further.

At the very least, what you have in your hands is a collection of classic recipes from our very own food heritage.

Sylvia Tan
September 2003

CONTENTS

THE CANTONESE BANQUET
Revolutions in dining out   **49**

STREET FOOD
The proof of loyal customers   **69**

SINGAPORE FUSION
Mixing and matching   95

ETHNIC SUPERMARKET
A new era in Singapore eating   117

Appendix

WHEN A PERANAKAN GENTLEMAN can ask for a chateaubriand steak to be cooked in his own kitchen in the 1930s, it is clear that the British colonial era of the nineteenth and early twentieth centuries left a strong culinary heritage in Singapore. It is a heritage that remains till today.

Chateaubriand (an extra-thick cut of fillet steak) remains an option at most western restaurants in town as well as spinach soup and possibly, even coffee glace (ice-cream with coffee sauce to us) which that same gentleman, Mr Lee Chim Huk, also ordered back then. He was also the one who took his family out for ice-creams every Sunday at Raffles Cafe, part of the pre-war Raffles Hotel complex, and hosted family dinners at the Seaview Hotel, now demolished, where the menu could well have been roast beef with all its trimmings.

These are dishes we take for granted today, but they would have been strange and unusual foods then for the Singapore population, aside from the ilk of Mr Lee and his family, that is. For in the nineteenth and even the early twentieth centuries, Asians lived socially segregated from the colonials. They were banned from the many social clubs existing then, a ban that continued until the early 60s, and seldom visited the hotels at which much of wining and dining of the era took place. But if they did visit the Raffles, Goodwood, Adelphi and the Prince's Hotel Garni, they would have noticed that western food was the order of the day at these primarily white establishments. In the 1940s, only the Cathay Hotel had a Chinese restaurant and much later, the Cockpit Hotel served a legendary Rijstaffel.

They attempted to reproduce the dishes of the old country, albeit with some adjustments, depending on the ingredients that were available.

Despite such segregation, the food the colonials ate filtered down to the Asian population, thanks mainly to the cooks they employed, Hainanese cookboys who learnt how to prepare western standards such as roast chicken, mutton chops, pies and butter cakes according to their English mem's specific instructions. They attempted to reproduce the dishes of the old country, albeit with some adjustments, depending on the ingredients that were available. Thus, it was inevitable that oriental seasonings such as soya sauce found their way into western recipes and vice versa. It was just as inevitable for cooking here to be influenced by India, that other British colony at the time, as evidenced by the Indian curries and such dishes that became part of the Singapore table from very early on.

In the 1900s, the still new Cold Storage which was starting up its food retail business, began importing more and more new foods such as butter, milk, cheese, tomato sauce and frozen meats, making it possible for those interested in copying the eating habits of the colonials to do so. In 1930, Cold Storage started making quality bread on a large scale and recipes incorporating bread soon appeared.

Outside the domestic kitchens, the social clubs ended up the keepers of culinary tradition as they

A soup tureen from the Europe Hotel which operated till 1932 in an Edwardian building at the site of the old Supreme Court, now part of the National Art Gallery.

provided a style of European eating to a homesick population that yearned for the social habits they knew back home. At the Tanglin Club, the Singapore Swimming Club and the Singapore Cricket Club, for example, it became possible to indulge in the thoroughly British practice, of eating eggs, cured meats such as ham and bacon and bread for breakfast, of taking time out during the day for tea, cake and perhaps a sandwich, and of relaxing at sundown with a stiff whiskey and soda or a gin and tonic and some *makan kechil* (finger food).

In fact, you can still detect the flavour of those days from perusing today's club menus, which remain largely unchanged except perhaps for a stronger Asian component. Back then, it was strictly western with perhaps a few token Asian offerings such as fried mah mee and nasi goreng. But western ways were here to stay especially when it was perceived to be socially advantageous to learn the ways of the colonials.

An old photograph of a dinner party held at home in the 1930s by a well-to-do Chinese family saw crystalware and English china on the table and the male guests dressed in tuxedos. The women, however, still kept to their traditional oriental garb. In the 50s, it became fashionable to celebrate weddings with a tea reception, offering tea and coffee, cake and sandwiches and curry puffs, rather than a Chinese dinner. To encourage eating out at western restaurants, set lunches were later introduced where a menu of three or four courses was offered especially to office workers, making it easier for the customers to order and the kitchen to cater. The idea of serving food in a buffet spread came soon after, changing yet again the Asian way of eating round a table, with everybody sharing dishes.

All these were significant milestones, for from this period, can we trace the beginnings of our taste for thoroughly English foods such as shepherd's pie, sherry trifle and cream puffs. Indeed the influence is more extensive than we think — for today, we eat bread for breakfast, may opt for a sandwich for lunch and may well dine out on a steak without a thought as to how such practices all started. Stews, albeit adapted to local tastes with *sambal belacan* and soya sauces, can be said to be standard fare in many home kitchens and who has not sat down for curry tiffin at one of the social clubs, which still serves it to an old-fashioned T? In fact, the new refurbished and six-star Raffles Hotel still offers a lavish spread of curries with all its traditional trimmings at its Tiffin Room where the past splendour of the colonies can be tasted even now.

PEPPER STEAK [For 6]

This is the steak we grew up with at steakhouses run by Hainanese cooks who learnt kitchen secrets from the British and the Peranakan Chinese. Powerful with pepper and rich with butter, it would arrive at the table on cow-shaped cast-iron platters.

6 rump or sirloin steaks, about 150-200 g each
4 tsps black peppercorns
1 clove garlic
3 tbs olive oil
$1/_4$ cup finely chopped shallots
4 tbs butter
1 cup beef stock
Salt to taste

Trim fat off the steaks and pat dry with kitchen towels. Coarsely crush peppercorns in a plastic bag, using a rolling pin, or pound them in a mortar. Cut garlic clove into half. Rub meat surface with cut garlic.

Brush steaks all over with oil. Press crushed peppercorns onto meat surface. Do the same for the other side. Sprinkle some salt over steaks.

Heat 1 tb oil in a cast-iron pan over medium-high heat. Sear steaks for 3 minutes on either side for medium rare. Remove pan from heat and reserve drippings. Place steaks on plates, cover with foil to keep warm while you make the sauce.

Return the pan to medium heat and add 1 tb butter to drippings in pan. Saute shallots till translucent, add stock and boil till gravy is reduced by half. Add rest of the butter, whisk with a fork to emulsify and pour over steaks.

HAM STEAK WITH PINEAPPLE [For 6]

Thanks to tinned pineapple, ham and pineapple became a classic combination. Cubes of ham and pineapple on a toothpick became a favourite *makan kechil* (finger food) while ham steaks topped with a glazed pineapple slice were featured on coffee house menus.

6 slices of 2-cm thick ham
6 tinned pineapple rings
$1/_2$ cup pineapple syrup
$1/_2$ tsp mustard powder
1 tsp honey
1 tbs butter

Remove rind and snip fat at intervals to prevent ham steaks from curling. Heat grill. When hot, grill steaks at medium heat for 10-15 minutes, turning once. Remove steaks and place on plate.

Mix mustard powder, honey and pineapple juice in a bowl. Heat butter in a pan, brown pineapple rings, turning once. Pour on juice mixture and heat till bubbling. Place browned pineapple rings on steaks. Pour on pan juices and serve immediately.

BUTTER-RUBBED ROAST CHICKEN

[For 4-6]

1 capon (about 1$^1/_2$ kg, 3 lb)
1 tbs butter
Salt and pepper to taste

Gravy:
1 tsp plain flour
1 chicken stock cube
1 cup water

Heat oven to 200°C. Wash chicken in several changes of water. Dry outside and cavity with paper towels.

Rub butter all over chicken, then sprinkle salt and pepper over the bird. Place in a roasting pan and roast, basting once or twice with pan juices, for about 1 hour (20 minutes for every 500 g) or till juices run clear when pierced in the thickest part of the thigh. If there is any trace of blood, the chicken is not ready.

To ensure moistness, cook chicken on its side and only turn it breast side up in the last 10 minutes to brown.

When done, remove chicken to serving plate. Pour off excess fat from roasting pan. Add flour, water and stock cube to pan and heat directly on the stove, stirring till gravy is thickened. Adjust seasoning. Strain gravy into a sauce boat and serve on the side.

POTATO SALAD

[For 4]

$^1/_2$ kg (1 lb) potatoes
1 large onion
1 stick celery
1 bunch parsley
1 cup of chopped ham
$^1/_2$ cup mayonnaise
Pepper to taste

Scrub potatoes clean. Cook unpeeled potatoes in a pot of salted water till tender but not falling apart. Peel and cut into 2 cm cubes.

Peel onion and remove fiberous part of celery. Roughly chop onion and celery. Chop parsley finely. Add chopped vegetables to the potatoes. Mix well with the mayonnaise and top with ham and lots of black pepper.

Believe it or not, a simple roast chicken was a treat back in the 1950s, for few owned an oven back then. For a luscious, golden chicken, flavour did not rely on herbs nor garlic, but simple decadent butter.

Another old favourite was the potato salad. It became, and still is, a party standard especially at barbecues and picnics. And it had to be creamy - vinaigrette dressing was unheard of then - with lots of sweet raw onions and possibly, some ham.

CHICKEN STEW [For 6]

A convenient one-pot meal quickly adopted by Asian families. They added their own touches, however, to this quintessential Western casserole, such as sambal chilli and soya sauce.

1 chicken (about $1^1/_2$ kg, 3 lb)
2 large purple onions, peeled and cut into quarters
2 carrots, peeled and cut into chunks
3 potatoes, peeled and cut into chunks
300 g (10 oz) frozen peas (optional)
$1/_3$ cup flour
Salt and pepper to taste
1 tsp dark soya sauce
2 tbs vegetable oil
1 small stick cinnamon
3 cloves

Wash chicken in several changes of water. Cut into 6-8 pieces. Season flour with salt and papper and coat chicken pieces with it.

Heat 2 tbs vegetable oil in hot pan. Brown coated chicken pieces, turning over once. Remove. Brown onions, then the potatoes. Return chicken to the pot. Add water to just cover the chicken and simmer for $1^1/_2$ hours with a stick of cinnamon and cloves or till chicken is tender. Add carrots halfway through. If using peas, add in the last few minutes.

If stew is too light, add dark soya sauce to darken colour. Taste and adjust seasoning, if required.

MINCE WITH POTATOES AND PEAS [For 4-6]

It may be basic mince to an Englishman, but to the Singaporean, this is comfort food indeed. In the Singapore version, the beef mince has been changed to pork, while cinnamon and cloves scent the mix and soya sauce adds the final flourish. The Goanese have a similar dish called *quema*, as do the Indians their *kheema*.

500 g (1 lb) pork mince (or beef)
1 large onion, peeled and chopped
2 potatoes, peeled and cut into cubes
250 g (8 oz) frozen peas
1 tsp dark soya sauce
1 tsp salt or to taste
1 small stick cinnamon
3 cloves
A dash of pepper
2 tbs vegetable oil

Heat oil in a hot pan. Saute onions till soft and fragrant. Add mince and break up meat with a fork to brown.

Add potatoes, cinnamon and cloves. Season with soya sauce, salt and pepper. Stir well. Add $1/_2$ cup of water and bring to simmering point to soften potatoes.

When potatoes are tender, add peas. Mix well. Taste and adjust seasoning. If it is too dry, add a splash of water.

The Chinese have their own version of Chicken Stew and, of course, they ate it with rice!

EGG SALAD [For 6]

The arrival of bottled mayonnaise led to salads being part of the Singapore table and they were all creamy. The egg salad was the simplest. Here we are not talking about the American chopped egg salad, but merely sliced hardboiled egg, seasoned with salt and pepper and slathered with mayonnaise. It was so simple, it had no business to taste so good – but it did!

4-6 eggs
1 cucumber, peeled and sliced
2 tomatoes, sliced
$^1/_2$ onion, sliced
Heart of an iceberg lettuce
$^1/_2$ cup mayonnaise, bottled or home-made
Salt and pepper to taste

Boil eggs in a pot of cold water. When eggs are cooked, plunge them in cold water to make peeling them easier.

Wet knife before slicing eggs. Wash and dry tender lettuce leaves.

Place egg, sliced onion, cucumber and tomato on a bed of lettuce leaves. Season with salt and pepper. Pour over dressing, which can be salad cream, mayonnaise or later, Thousand Island Dressing.

SHEPHERD'S PIE [For 6-8]

The Eurasian community especially embraced this versatile British dish which traditionally is made with lamb, since it is, after all, a shepherd's pie. In Singapore however, it is more often made with beef mince and is again flavoured with cinnamon and cloves, quite unlike the original straight-ahead recipe.

1 onion, chopped
2 carrots, grated
2 celery sticks, chopped
2 tbs vegetable oil
500 g (1 lb) minced meat
1 stick of cinnamon
3 cloves
1 cup beef stock
1 tbs flour
1 kg (2 lb) potatoes
1 tbs milk
60 g (2 oz) butter
Salt and pepper
Extra butter

Heat oil in a pan and saute onion till soft. Fry the vegetables. Add the meat, breaking it up with a fork, then the cinnamon stick and cloves. Add the stock, sprinkle over with flour, and simmer till meat sauce thickens. Season with salt and pepper to taste and leave aside.

Place potatoes in a pot of salted water and cook till tender. Drain. When cool, peel and mash potato, using a fork. Add salt, pepper, butter and milk to the mash and stir well to make it smooth and creamy.

Place mince mixture in a shallow baking tray and cover evenly with potato. Smoothen and score surface with a fork. Dot with bits of butter. Brown for 10 to 15 minutes in a hot oven, 220˚C or till top is golden. Serve hot or cold.

HOME-MADE MAYONNAISE

Although everyone relied on bottled mayonnaise then, the taste of freshly made mayonnaise cannot be beaten. You need two egg yolks, salt and white pepper to taste, 400 ml olive oil and juice of half a lemon. Using a wire whisk, beat egg yolks, salt and pepper in a bowl till thick and smooth. Drizzle oil and lemon juice into the mixture and continue whisking until mayonnaise is thick and glossy. Taste and adjust seasoning. Thin down with warm water if needed.

THOUSAND ISLAND DRESSING

It was a creamy salad dressing that originated in New York in the early 1900s and it became a hit in Singapore in the 1960s. A mayonnaise-based dressing, we enjoyed the pink bottled version yet it is easy to make up. You just add bottled tomato and chilli sauces to salad cream in the proportion of 1:2 and add some chopped gherkins for crunch.

MULLIGATAWNY SOUP [For 6-8]

Another Anglo-Indian dish. *Mulaga* means pepper and *tanni* means water or broth, hence "peppery broth" is a good translation. Over time, it became a curried soup. The English version even has chopped apples and root vegetables in the pot, but in Singapore, a stripped-down yet gutsy version is served.

    1 small chicken, about 500 g (1 lb)
    2-3 tbs meat curry powder
    1 onion, chopped
    2 cloves garlic, chopped
    1 cup coconut milk
    Lemon juice
    1 tbs salt
    Fried shallots for garnish
    1 cup cooked rice

Boil whole chicken in a pot filled with 6 cups of water. When cooked, cool and remove flesh to shred. Return bones to the pot and continue boiling for another 15-20 minutes. Strain stock. Leave aside for use later.

Heat 1 tbs. oil in another pot and saute onion, garlic and curry powder till oil rises. Add chicken stock and salt. Bring to the boil and taste. Adjust seasoning if needed. Stri in coconut milk. Add a squeeze of lemon juice.

To serve, place some shredded chicken and 1 tbs cooked rice in a bowl and pour hot curried soup over. Garnish with fried shallots.

FISH MOOLIE [For 6]

This is a spicy fish and coconut dish, which probably has its roots in Portuguese cuisine. (The word *mohlyu* is Portuguese for gravy.) There is also an Indian dish called *molee* as well as an Eurasian and Malay moolie and they all share common ingredients such as turmeric, shrimp paste and yes, coconut milk.

    6 fish steaks (snapper, mackerel or threadfin)
    1 large onion, sliced
    1 knob ginger, cut into strips

    Spice paste:
    3 tbs galangal powder (or 4 slices of fresh galangal)
    1 tsp turmeric powder
    4 buah keras (candlenuts)
    2 stalks lemon grass (use white part only)
    1 tsp shrimp paste

    500 ml (2 cups) coconut milk
    1 tbs vinegar
    1 tsp sugar
    1 tsp salt

    Garnish:
    Fried sliced shallots
    Fried sliced garlic
    Fried red and green chilli strips

Process spice paste ingredients till fine in a chopper. Sear fish steaks in a frying pan, using just 1-2 tbs oil. Set aside.

Add another tablespoon of oil in the pan, heat and fry onion and ginger till browned. Saute spice paste, then add coconut milk. Heat gently, stirring continuously till it comes to the boil. Season to taste with vinegar, salt and sugar.

Add fried fish, heat through gently and serve with garnishes of fried chilli, shallots and garlic.

CURRY TIFFIN [For 8-10]

A tradition carried over from the days of the British Raj. This Anglo-Indian practice of having curry and attendant trimmings for lunch (*tiffin* is the Indian word for lunch) became a tradition here, especially at the social clubs. Such a meal would have a curry as the centrepiece and an assortment of side dishes that were as interesting as the main course.

2 chickens (about 1¹/₂ kg, 3 lb each)
    OR 1¹/₂ kg (3 lb) of stewing beef
1 onion, chopped
1 knob of ginger, chopped
2 cloves of garlic, chopped
4 tomatoes, chopped
1 cinnamon stick
4-5 cloves
¹/₂ cup meat curry powder
500 ml (2 cups) coconut milk
6-8 potatoes, peeled and cut into large pieces
4 tbs vegetable oil
2 tbs salt and pepper to taste

Wash chickens in several changes of water. Chop each bird into eight to 10 pieces. Dry with paper towels.

Heat oil in a pot. Brown onions, garlic and ginger, then add the curry powder, made first into a paste with a little water, and the cinnamon, cloves, onion, garlic and ginger.

Brown the chicken pieces, then the potatoes. Add tomato and enough water to reach halfway of the chicken. Season wth salt and pepper. Bring to the boil, then turn down the fire to simmer till chicken and potatoes are tender.

When potatoes are done, add coconut milk. Stir constantly till curry comes again to a gentle boil. Taste again to adjust seasoning, if necessary.

Serve this curry with rice and all or some of the following items: sweet mango chutney, pineapple, cucumber and onion salad, hardboiled salted egg, fried bombay duck (a kind of dried fish), sliced apples, kropok (prawn crackers) and/or nuts.

"Add raisins to any curry recipe and you will find that they improve it a great deal!"
~ *Country Women's Association of Western Australia Cookery Book and Household Hints*

SAMBAL SANDWICH FILLING

[Makes 2 small jars]

The sandwich is an import although the Asian population did eat bread but mostly for breakfast, and then it was bread and condensed milk or kaya, or bread, butter and sometimes, sugar, dunked into sweet black coffee.

Sandwiches were served only at Western-style food establishments or at colonial hotels. They could also be found at tea receptions, highly popular in the 1950s to celebrate weddings and birthdays.

When a new way of eating took hold, we created our own sandwich fillings that are probably not found any-where else in the world. Indeed in the 1960s, it became *de rigeuer* to serve sambal sandwiches at dance parties.

> 300 g (10 oz) dried prawn
> 5 fresh red chillies
> 3 dried red chillies
> $^1/_2$ cup shallots, peeled
> Pinch of salt
> 1 tsp sugar

Wash dried prawns and soak for just five minutes in hot water to soften. Too long a soak would strip the prawns of flavour. Save soaking water. Soak dried chillies in hot water to soften. Process dried prawn in a food chopper until fine. Remove, then process the chillies and onion to similar texture.

Heat 4 tbs oil in a wok and saute spice paste gently, mois-tening now and then with shrimp water, till soft and fragrant. Add dried prawn. Continue frying over slow fire till mixture dries out and turns golden brown.

You can also brown the shrimp mixture in a slow oven. Stir once or twice during roasting. Remove when done and cool. Store in a dry jar in the fridge where it can keep for months.

Shortcut: You can replace the chillies and onions with 2 tbs of bottled sambal chilli paste and continue as above.

CORNED BEEF SANDWICHES

[For 10]

> 1 tin corned beef
> 1 onion
> 2 red chillies

Peel and slice onion. Slice red chillies. Use fork to flake the corned beef from the tin. Heat 1 tbs oil in a wok and saute onions till soft and translucent. Add the flaked corned beef and continue to fry, stirring briskly till the meat browns in parts. Add chillies. Mix well and use as sandwich filling.

To sliced sandwich bread, crusts trimmed, you could spread fillings such as:

Egg - Mashed hardboiled egg, chopped celery, salt and pepper to taste, moistened into a paste with mayonnaise or salad cream.

Sardine - Tinned sardines, chopped raw onion, chillies and lime juice, all mashed into a paste.

Chicken - Shredded roast chicken, lots of salt and pepper on buttered bread.

CHEESE STRAWS

[Makes 48-60 straws]

Out of fashion now, but they were popular party food in the 1950s. While cheese was not a favourite food with the Asian population, these baked cheese pastries and grilled cheese on toast were popular snacks.

> 100 g (1 cup) flour
> 75 g ($^1/_2$ cup) grated cheese
> 75 g ($^1/_3$ cup) butter
> 1 egg, separated
> Pinch of salt
> Pinch of paprika
> 1 tsp cold water

Rub flour into butter in a basin till it resembles breadcrumbs. Add egg yolk, cheese, salt, pepper, paprika and enough water to bind. Roll out dough on floured board to get 5 mm-thick sheet. Cut into finger-length straws.

Place on baking sheet and brush with egg white. Bake in 200˚C oven for 8-10 minutes. Remove and cool on wire tray.

SAGO PUDDING

[For 6-8]

According to Singapore cookbook doyen Mrs Ellice Handy, this pudding is also known as Singapore, Penang, Malacca or Straits Settlement pudding. Supposedly a Malay recipe, sago milk puddings can also be found in English cuisine. In the Singapore version, however, coconut milk and palm sugar replace the milk and sugar in the English recipe. It became *the* dessert after a curry tiffin.

2 cups small sago pearls
2 egg whites
Salt
2 cups coconut milk
1 tsp corn flour
300 g (10 oz) gula melaka (palm sugar)
$1^1/_2$ cups water
Pandan leaf

Wash briskly sago pearls. Bring a pot of water to boil. When water boils, add drained sago pearls, stirring constantly. Cook for 10 minutes, turn off fire and leave till pearls turn translucent. Drain using a large strainer and wash away the starch under the cold tap. Set aside.

Whisk egg whites stiff and frothy. Add pinch of salt. Fold whites into drained sago. Pour into a large mould or six to eight small ones. Cool in refrigerator.

Heat coconut milk in a pot. Stir in corn flour, made first into a paste with some water, stirring over gentle heat till sauce thickens. Add a pinch of salt and store in refrigerator.

Place gula melaka into a pot. Add $1^1/_2$ water. Heat, together with a knotted pandan leaf, till gula malacca dissolves. Allow syrup to reduce to about 1 cup.

Place a plate over mould, upturn pudding onto plate. Serve with coconut milk and palm syrup for guests to help themselves to.

SHERRY TRIFLE

[For 10]

This old English dessert has long been taken over by the Eurasian community. Thanks to them, it remains popular in Singapore, even if it was then made with custard powder and tinned fruit! In this recipe, fresh fruit replaces the tinned fruit though sherry still spikes the soaked cake.

300 g (10 oz) sponge cake (or butter cake or sugee cake)
4 tbs sherry
1 punnet fresh strawberries
60 g ($1/_2$ cup) caster sugar plus 2 tbs sugar
2 cups milk
2 tbs corn flour
8 egg yolks
Chinese nut brittle, broken up
200 ml ($^3/_4$ cup) cream
1 vanilla pod, optional

Cut up cake and place pieces in a glass bowl. Sprinkle sherry evenly over the cake. Hull strawberries. Cut berries into half and scatter over cake. Sprinkle 2 tbs sugar over fruit. Leave aside.

To make the custard, place yolks into a basin. Whisk till creamy with rest of the combined sugar. Mix corn flour in a couple of spoonfuls from the cold milk to make a paste.

Heat rest of the milk in another basin together with a vanilla pod, if using. When heated but not boiling, pour milk into the egg yolk mixture.

Stir in the corn flour paste and keep stirring over a low flame till custard coats the back of a wooden spoon, about 20 minutes. It should not boil. Remove vanilla pod, if using.

Keep stirring especially when custard starts to thicken, but if it does get lumpy, you can still use a wire whisk to work out the lumps.

Pour hot custard over the fruit and cake. Allow it to set a couple of hours in the refrigerator. To serve, whip a carton of cream till it forms soft peaks. Pour cream over the trifle, scatter broken nut brittle over and serve.

BREAD PUDDING
[For 10]

Again we have to thank the Eurasian community for ensuring that this basically English recipe is part of our culinary tradition. In their households, such a pudding is made regularly. Today, however, almost all the racial groups make bread puddings. While there are differences in the recipes, they all make use of leftover bread and custard.

5-6 slices leftover bread, cut into squares
Butter
4 eggs
4 cups milk
Half cup sugar
$^1/_2$ cup raisins
Pinch of cinnamon powder

Butter bread slices. Beat eggs, sugar and milk with a whisk until sugar dissolves.

Place buttered bread in a greased baking dish, 20 X 20 cm. Pour custard over. Press down bread to soak up the custard. Scatter raisins over. Leave for about 15 minutes.

Heat oven to 180°C. Cover baking dish with foil and place the dish in a large roasting pan. Fill pan with hot water to about 5 cm from the top of the dish. Bake for about 30 minutes or till custard sets. Remove foil and continue to bake for about another 15 minutes to brown the top.

COCONUT CANDY
[Makes 24]

At one time, you could find it for sale at almost every fun fair - yet they are not unique to us. A cooked concoction of grated coconut sugar and milk is common to countries such as the Caribbean, Guam, Puerto Rico and significantly, India and Africa... all places where coconuts can be found in abundance.

3 cups sugar
1 cup evaporated milk
3 tightly packed cups grated coconut (skin removed)
1 tbs butter
A pinch salt
1 tsp vanilla essence
A few drops of food colouring
    OR 3 dessertspoons cocoa powder

In a saucepan, boil sugar and milk over medium heat until it becomes a thin syrup. Add coconut and butter, stirring constantly to prevent burning. The mixture is ready when it thickens and begins to pulls away from side of pan. Test by dropping a small piece into cold water. It should harden immediately.

Stir in cocoa while it is still boiling, if you want a chocolate candy or else stir in a few drops of food colouring at the last minute.

Spread mixture over a buttered tray. Cut into pieces while still warm, and leave to harden.

BUTTER CAKE [About 15 servings]

3 cups plain flour
1 tsp baking powder
$^1/_4$ tsp salt
150 g ($^2/_3$ cup) unsalted butter
2 cups sugar
4 large eggs, lightly beaten
1 cup milk
1 tsp vanilla essence

Position rack in the lower third of the oven and preheat to 180˚C. Line a round cake tin with wax paper and grease with butter. Sift flour, baking powder, and salt into a bowl. Set aside.

Cream butter and sugar on medium speed of a mixer, stopping occasionally to scrape down the sides of the bowl, until the mixture is very light in color and texture, 4 to 5 minutes.

Gradually pour in the eggs, about a tablespoon at a time, beating well after each addition. (If the mixture looks curdled, add a little flour.) Continue beating until the mixture is ivory-coloured.

Fold in the flour mixture lightly, but thoroughly. Add the milk if it looks too stiff. Finally add the vanilla essence. Pour the batter evenly in the prepared tin.

Bake for 10 minutes, the reduce heat to 160˚C to bake for another 45-50 minutes or until the top springs back when the cake is lightly pressed. Insert a stick into the centre. If it comes out clean, the cake is ready.

Note: To make butter cake in tubes, collect 10-12 hotdog sausage tins. Line the tins with wax paper, allowing it to extend about 3 cm (approx 1 inch) above the top of the tins. Grease the paper with butter, fill the tins with batter just beyond the rims and bake.

Probably the first Western cake that Singaporeans made. It originated from the British recipe for pound cake, which uses a pound of flour, butter, eggs and sugar. Bakers would also know it as the 1-2-3-4 cake, that is 1 cup butter, 2 cups sugar, 3 cups flour and 4 eggs!

Good Bread needs good butter

Australian Butter!

Bread and Butter complete your meal
SINGAPORE COLD STORAGE CO., LTD.

BANANA CAKE

[About 10 servings]

This was a favourite offering at school and church fun fairs and tea parties in the 1950s. You hardly find it these days, so homespun is its appeal. Yet it is a great way to use up overripe bananas.

115 g ($^1/_2$ cup) butter
1 cup sugar
2 eggs
1 tsp vanilla essence
1 cup mashed banana, about 3 pieces
2 cups flour
1 tsp baking powder
$^1/_2$ tsp salt
$^1/_3$ cup milk or buttermilk

Cream together butter and sugar. Add mashed banana, eggs, and vanilla essence. Combine well.

Sift together dry ingredients. Add flour mixture to the banana mixture, alternately with milk. Blend well.

Pour into a greased and floured loaf pan (oblong pan). Bake at 160°C degrees for 75 minutes, Insert toothpick into the centre of the cake. If it comes out clean, the cake is done.

CREAM PUFFS

[About 3 dozen puffs]

Who could forget cream, or rather custard, puffs eaten at the Polar Café? It was a special treat and we all grew up with this memory. Again, a British legacy with its use of powdered custard powder, we actually prefer it to the fresh cream-filled puffs that have now come on the market.

BASIC CHOUX PASTRY
1 cup water
115 g ($^1/_2$ cup) unsalted butter
$^1/_4$ tsp salt
1 tsp sugar
1 cup flour
4 large eggs

Preheat oven to 180°C. Put water, salt, sugar and butter into saucepan and bring to a boil over medium heat. When boiling, immediately put in all the flour. Stir with a wooden spoon until flour forms into a ball and leaves the sides of the pot. Cool.

In the meantime, lightly grease two cookie sheets. Place dough in the mixing bowl of an electric mixer. With mixer running at medium speed, add eggs one at a time, blending well each time. Mixture should look smooth and glossy at the end.

Spoon out balls, using two teaspoons, onto the tray. Bake until golden brown, about 20 minutes. Switch off heat and leave for five minutes more in the oven, with the door left open for pastry to dry out inside.

Remove from oven and cool on a wire rack. Make a slit at the side of each puff to fill with vanilla custard later or freeze for later use.

VANILLA CUSTARD
4 egg yolks
$^1/_4$ cup corn flour
Pinch of salt
$^1/_2$ cup sugar
2 cups milk
1 tsp vanilla essence

Mix egg yolks, corn flour, salt, half of the sugar and $^1/_2$ cup of the milk in a bowl, blending well. In a saucepan, heat the rest of the milk and sugar together. When it comes to a boil, whisk in the egg yolk mixture. Cook over a low fire, whisking all the time to prevent burning. When mixture thickens, remove from heat.

Leave for 2-3 minutes, then stir in vanilla essence. Cool, then cover surface of custard with plastic wrap to prevent it from forming a 'skin'.

Place in refrigerator to set. Before using, beat custard with an electric beater to get a smooth creamy finish. Fill puffs.

Note: Versions of this custard can also be found in Italy and France. It can be made up to two days ahead.

MARBLE CAKE [About 15 servings]

Before chocolate cake, Singaporeans loved their marble cake, which is a butter cake with swirls of cocoa. Again it was a recipe inherited from the British.

225 g (1 cup) butter
$1^1/_2$ cups sugar
4 eggs
1 cup milk
$3^1/_4$ cups flour
1 tbs baking powder
Pinch of salt
$^1/_4$ cup unsweetened cocoa powder

Preheat oven to 180°C. Grease and flour a 15 cm round cake tin. In a large bowl, cream butter with sugar. Beat in eggs, then the milk.

In another bowl, mix flour, baking powder and salt. Fold in flour mixture into the creamed mixture. Pour out half of the batter into another bowl and stir in the cocoa. Using a spoon, add the light and dark batters in layers in the cake tin and then swirl slightly with a knife.

Bake the cake for about 70 minutes, or until a skewer comes out clean when inserted into the centre of the cake. Transfer to a rack to cool.

The Hainanese Connection

SNACK BAR – THE NAME ITSELF IS AMERICAN. After World War II **and** with the rise of victorious America, the days of hamburgers and soda pop were to hit Singapore. You could call these small intimate establishments, soda fountains, creameries or milk bars, but the menus were more or less the same and they were run mostly by the Hainanese, who seemed to hold the kitchen secrets of both western and Peranakan households of the time.

The best Chinese cooks then were employed by both groups to man the home kitchens and they learnt how to turn out both western and Peranakan dishes from their English mems and their nonya lady bosses. A dab hand at seasonings, they soon grasped how to improve the flavour of a stew say, with soya sauce and perhaps . And when the openings for full-time cooks at households dried up after the war, they went into business for themselves, selling, what else, the food they learnt how to cook at their previous employers' homes. They (and a few Westerners) set up restaurants serving westernised food in western style, complete with china, knives and forks and starched folded napkins.

But such touches aside, the food they cooked was actually Asianised western food – Hainanese pork chops, for example, are nothing like the English thick cut pork chops with apple sauce on the side. And the Asian dishes on the menu would understandably be Peranakan-influenced, such as sambal prawns and sambal pomfret, chap chye and roti babi.

> *Who cannot recall the hip hangouts of the 1960s — the two Magnolia Milk Bars where young people used to meet up over an ice cream.*

Some of these old establishments still exist today. You can get old-fashioned eating at Hainanese-run eating places like The Ship (oxtail stews!) and Mooi Chin Restaurant, previously sited opposite the old Odeon cinema where one could eat in charming dark wood dining booths, complete with hat racks, and is now an air-conditioned generic dining room at Funan Centre. And then there is the famous Polar Café which still sells their curry and custard puffs, even franchising these decades-old pastries to other opera-tors, not forgetting (Stanley) Fosters Steakhouse, previously at Amber Arcade, now at the Holland Village, where you can still order a Fillet Fantastique, on a bed of crisp onions and topped with mushrooms, and Carpetbag Steak with oysters spilling out of a pocket in the meat. Another establishment is Berkely Cafe at Sloane's Court Hotel along Balmoral Road, where the restaurant is housed in a charming black and white mock Tudor building. Here, you will find standards like Chicken Maryland.

Other names live on only in our memories — who cannot recall the hip hangouts of the 1960s — the two Magnolia Milk Bars, one along Orchard Road and the other at the old Capitol cinema at Stamford Road, where young people used to meet over an ice cream before the international hotel chains and its 24-hour coffee houses set up shop?

Older folks would also remember a slew of English pub-type places along the Orchard Road belt of which Fosters has already been mentioned. They include the Pavilion where Specialist Centre now stands,

[Right] High Street and Polar Cafe, 1964.

Stella D'oro, even the quaint Tangle Inn where the décor was olde English right down to its dark wood gables and windows with diamond-shaped panes! At these places, English pub fare such as fish and chips, cottage pies, bangers and mash (mashed potatoes and sausages) and mixed grills were offered.

Grilled meats truly reached its heights of popularity when American-type steak houses opened in the 1970s. At the Cairnhill and Emerald Steak Houses, we learnt how to eat huge slabs of sizzling meat served on cast iron platters and even to stipulate its degree of doneness. The height of style must have been Fosters' charming practice of sticking little flags into the meat indicating its cooked state.

This American craze was already foreshadowed by the popularity of stylish Mont D'or Café at the old Ngee Ann Building, the precursor of Ngee Ann City. It became the in-place in the 1960s — where teenagers thronged to buy its chocolate éclairs, yet another food craze to hit Singapore. Others were to come along — the chicken pies and ice-cream sundaes at Honeyland Milk Bar and the nasi padang lunches at GH Café, both along Battery Road. Outside town, families and young people would frequent Tay Buan Guan Café in Katong for its ice-cream sodas, the Red House, as well as the fairy-lighted Wonderland restaurant where one could partake of a fairly posh western meal, often starting with the ever so elegant prawn cocktail, at less than posh prices.

The American influence was undeniable. It was de riguer for any self-respecting snack bar to serve American foods such as hot dogs with all the trimmings, hamburgers, club sandwiches and several kinds of ice-cream specialities.

Some places however went totally against the trend and Singaporeans began an unusual but lasting love affair with Russian food. Introduced by a white Russian woman who came to Singapore in the 1960s, Mummy Liber is credited with teaching Singaporeans how to cook dishes such as Mongolian steak, shashlik and borscht soup in the kitchen of the White Bear restaurant in Bras Basah Road. Her students proved to be avid learners for they went on to open the highly successful and sophisticated Troika Restaurant in Liat Towers and DBS Building, when the White Bear closed down. Today, a new generation of Singaporeans still lap up these dishes now cooked by the descendants of the very Hainanese chefs Mummy Liber taught decades ago, but at their own establishments — Borscht at Serangoon Gardens and Shashlik at Far East Shopping Centre.

PRAWN COCKTAIL [For 4]

How chic it was in the 1960s to order a prawn cocktail. Basically prawns served with salad and a creamy dressing in a stemmed glass, it was pretty and elegant. This cold appetiser was found in many early menus in snack bars and especially in those Western restaurants run by the Hainanese.

8 medium-sized prawns
$^1/_2$ head iceberg lettuce
$^1/_2$ onion, chopped
1 stick celery, chopped

Dressing:
3 tbs cream
3 tbs mayonnaise
3 tbs tomato sauce
3 tbs Worcestershire sauce
$^1/_2$ tsp ground cayenne pepper
Salt and pepper
1 lemon, quartered

Bring a small pot of water to boil. Cook prawns in their shells till pink. Peel prawns. Combine cream, mayonnaise, tomato and Worchestershire sauces and mix well. Adjust seasoning to your liking.

Line four martini glasses with lettuce leaves, top with chopped onions and celery, then the prawns and a lemon wedge. Spoon on dressing. Serve chilled.

CHEF'S SALAD [For 4]

One of the earliest salads on the snack bar menu and everyone ate it, probably because there was lots of meat in it! American in origin, it was basically an assortment of cold meats and cheese, placed on top of a bed of greens and called a chef's salad because the chef uses whatever is on hand to create a main course salad.

4 slices each of turkey, ham, roast beef and Swiss cheese
1 small cucumber
2 tomatoes
$^1/_4$ head iceberg lettuce
$^1/_4$ head Romaine lettuce
$^1/_4$ head red cabbage, cut into strips
$^1/_2$ cup mayonnaise dressing

Stack turkey and cut in julienne strips. Repeat with ham, roast beef and Swiss cheese. Slice cucumber; cut tomatoes in wedges. Wash and tear lettuces into bite-sized pieces

Put lettuces on a serving plate. Top with cabbage, meats, cheese, cucumber and tomatoes. Serve with a creamy dressing which could be mayonnaise or Thousand Island dressing.

Optional: You could add chopped hardboiled egg and capers as garnishes.

HAMBURGERS [For 4]

The hamburger was introduced to the American public in 1904 at the St Louis World's Fair. It would take another 50 years for Burger King and McDonald's to appear in the US. But even before fast food arrived in Singapore, the hamburger was already popular among teenagers here.

250 g ($^1/_2$ lb) minced chuck beef
250 g ($^1/_2$ lb) minced sirloin beef
1 onion, chopped
1 egg
1 tsp salt
Pepper to taste
4 tsps butter
6 round soft buns
4 tomato slices
Raw onion rings

Mix minced meat together with chopped onion, egg, salt and a grind of black pepper. Shape into four thick patties. Chill in the fridge till firm.

Heat a fry pan over high heat. Sear patties for five minutes until browned, turn over and cook for another 1-2 minutes for a rare burger. Remove from pan.

Split buns into half. Grill, cut sides up. Place patty on the bottom half of the bun, top with 1 tsp butter, a tomato slice and some onion rings. Add a squeeze of tomato sauce, cover with the other half of the bun and serve at once.

HOT DOGS [For 10]

10 hot dog buns
10 hot dog suasages
3 tomatoes, sliced
2 onions, sliced
Mustard
Relish
Gherkin pickles
Butter
Tomato sauce

Take a bun, split it into half and grill it, cut side up. Butter it and fill with a boiled hot dog sausage. Load it with tomato slices, onions, mustard, relish, pickle and tomato sauce.

CURRY PUFFS [Makes 12]

Who can forget Polar Café curry puffs? They (and the equally famous custard puffs) were a treat any time at Polar Café, that white-tiled cake shop along High Street. Today, that humble curry puff has been franchised, making it convenient for anyone to enjoy this pastry, redolent with curried chicken and caramelised onions.

1 packet 375 g ($^3/_4$ lb) frozen puff pastry

Or make your own shortcrust pastry:
200 g (2 cups) flour
1 tsp salt
125 g ($^1/_2$ cup) butter, cut into small pieces
25 ml ($2^1/_2$ tbs) cold water
1 egg for egg wash

Filling:
$^1/_2$ chicken
1 tbs oil
2 large onions, chopped
1 tbs curry powder
1 tsp salt
Pepper to taste

To make short crust pastry, sieve flour and salt. Rub butter into flour till it resembles breadcrumbs. Add water slowly till mixture comes together into a dough. Knead it a few times and leave aside covered while you make the filling.

Preheat oven to 200°C. Grease baking tray using an oil or butter spray. Heat a pot of water and boil the chicken until it is just cooked. De-bone and cut the meat into cubes. You can freeze the broth for use later.

Heat the oil and saute onions until caramelised and fragrant. Add curry powder, pepper and salt and stir briskly. Add a little water to prevent burning. When spices are fragrant, add the chicken meat. Continue cooking until the mixture is almost dry. Set aside.

Roll out whichever dough you are using to about $^1/_2$ cm thick. Cut out circles with a diameter of 12 cm (use a Chinese rice bowl).

Put 1 tbs filling in the middle of each circle of dough. Fold to make a half moon, wet the edges with water and pinch close.

Place puffs onto baking tray. Brush tops with beaten egg and bake five minutes. Turn down the heat to 180°C and bake for another 20 minutes until golden brown.

Polar Puffs had their competition in what was popularly known as Rex curry puffs. Situated a toss away from the now closed Rex cinema, Old Chang Kee's version of the curry puff – deep fried, not baked – is a simple flour and water pastry stuffed with curried meat and half a hard-boiled egg.

SAUSAGE ROLLS [Makes 8]

Where can you buy sausage rolls these days? Fewer and fewer places. Popular once at Hainanese snack bars, they are almost phased out today. A pity, for the best of our sausage rolls was certainly more peppery and tasty than the original British counterpart.

200 g (7 oz) frozen puff pastry
8 pork sausages
1 small onion, chopped
1 egg
Pepper to taste

Heat oven to 200°C. Using oil or butter spray, grease the baking tray.

Skin the sausages and chop them. Add onion and lots of white pepper to sausage meat. Divide meat mixture into eight portions.

Roll out pastry to $^1/_2$ cm thick and cut into eight equal-sized squares. Shape meat mixture into rolls the length of the pastry squares.

Place each roll in the middle of a pastry square, dampen the edges of the pastry and roll till the edges meet. Pinch the edges together to secure them, but leave the ends of the rolls open.

Place the sausage rolls, seam side down, onto greased baking tray. Make slits on the top of each roll and brush tops with beaten egg.

Bake at 200°C for 10 minutes until pastry is well-risen. Reduce heat to 180C° and bake for a further 20 minutes till the pastry begins to brown. Remove and cool on a wire rack.

Note: To make sausage rolls using your own short crust pastry, see the recipe for Curry Puffs on the previous page.

CHICKEN PIES

[For 8-10]

Back in the 1960s, the best chicken pies were those made by the long gone Honeyland Milk Bar at Battery Road. But its heritage remains. Similar chicken pies — individual pies bulging with chicken, peas and carrots — are still available at clubs mainly where memories of bygone food still hold strong.

    1 packet 375 g ($^3/_4$ lb) frozen puff pastry
    2 tbs butter
    1 large onion
    600 g (1.1 lb) deboned chicken
    2 carrots
    2 potatoes
    2 cups green peas
    4 tbs flour
    Milk
    Salt and pepper to taste
    1 egg for egg wash

Cut the chicken into cubes. Chop the onion, peel potatoes and carrots and dice.

Heat the butter and brown the onions. Saute the diced chicken, then add diced vegetables and peas. Add water or milk to just cover the chicken and bring to the boil.

Add a little water to the flour to make a paste and add to the pan, stirring all the time till stew thickens. Season with salt and pepper to taste. Set aside.

Now preheat the oven to 200°C. Roll out the pastry to $^1/_2$ cm thick. Cut rounds to fit individual pie foil pans with about 1 cm overhang. Using a slotted spoon, fill pans with chicken filling. Top up with liquid.

Cut more rounds to exactly fit the top of the foil pans. Cover pans with these rounds and seal the edges with a fork. Brush the tops with beaten egg to glaze. Bake for 20-30 minutes or till golden brown.

Note: To make chicken pies your own short crust pastry, see the recipe for Curry Puffs on page 35.

BORSCHT [For 6]

This recipe may be of Russian origin, but it is as Singaporean as say, Chilli Crabs. Created by Hainanese chefs who had never been to Russia, its place in our food history is assured.

> 300 g (10 oz) shin beef
> 5 cups of water
> $^1/_4$ cup vegetable oil
> 1 large onion, chopped
> 1 carrot, sliced
> $^1/_4$ cabbage, shredded
> 3 large beets, peeled and grated
> 4 tomatoes, chopped
> 1 tbs salt
> 2 tbs red wine vinegar
> Black pepper, freshly ground
> $^1/_2$ cup sour cream

Cover shin beef with water, bring to the boil and cook till tender. Remove meat. Heat oil in a pot and brown onions. When softened, add sliced carrots and stir in the cabbage. Add strained meat stock to the pot and bring it to the boil. Add the beets, tomatoes, salt and pepper.

Cut the cooked beef into smaller pieces and add to the pot and cook for 15 minutes more. Season with red wine vinegar. Remove from heat and serve with a generous dollop of sour cream to each bowl.

BEEF SHASHLIK [For 4]

The White Bear restaurant in Bras Basah Road in the 1960s, the legendary Troika restaurant in the 1970s and 1980s, the Shashlik restaurant, still operating today – all served shashlik (or kebabs) and borscht as created by Chief Cook Yap Keng Swa. The Russian connection was Mummy Liber, a white Russian woman chef who also worked in the White Bear kitchen. While Russian shashlik uses lamb, in Singapore, it is beef.

> 500 gm (1 lb) sirloin beef or any cut of lean beef
>
> Marinade:
> 1 cup vegetable oil
> Juice from a lemon
> 1 clove garlic, chopped
> 1 onion, chopped
> 1 tsp salt
> Pepper to taste
> 1 bay leaf
> 1 tsp paprika
>
> Optional:
> 3 tomatoes
> 2 onions
> 2 green peppers

Cut beef into large cubes. Cut tomatoes and onions into quarters and peppers into squares. Leave aside.

Place beef in a bowl. Combine oil, lemon juice, salt, pepper, bay leaf, paprika, garlic, and onion. Pour over meat. Marinate, covered, in refrigerator overnight, turning occasionally. Thread beef and if using, tomato, onion and green pepper, on four long skewers.

Grill shashlik on medium barbecue 12-16 minutes, turning once. You can also place the skewers under the electric grill, on the topmost rung for 10 minutes, turning once for medium rare. During the cooking, baste meat and vegetables with additional marinade.

Strange as it sounds, Russian food in Singapore has a Hainanese connection. Hainanese chefs and waiters provided cuisine and service for the top tables for special family treats and businessmen closing deals.

OXTAIL STEW [For 6]

Actually a hearty European winter stew, it had no business finding a following in hot tropical Singapore, but it did and has remained so. It is still a favourite lunch special at those Hainanese eateries which use soya sauce and what else to flavour even western style dishes.

1 kg (2 lb) oxtail, trimmed
1 tsp dark soya sauce
$1/4$ cup flour
1 tsp salt
Black pepper
$1/4$ cup oil
1 onion, chopped
3 garlic cloves, chopped
1 cinnamon stick
4 cloves
2 tbs tomato puree
400 ml (1 $3/4$ cup) beef stock
2 tomatoes, quartered
1 carrot, cut into wedges
Light soya sauce, salt and black pepper to taste
Parsley, chopped

Place oxtail in a large bowl. Season with dark soya sauce. Marinate at least two hours.

Combine flour, salt and black pepper in a bowl. Dip marinated oxtail into flour mixture making sure it is coated thoroughly.

Heat oil and fry oxtail until lightly browned. Remove meat from pot, drain off all but 1-2 tablespoons oil. Add onion and garlic to pot and sauté lightly. Add cinnamon stick and cloves, then the beef stock and tomato puree. Stir.

Return meat to the pot and bring to the boil, then turn down the fire to simmer. Add carrot and tomatoes to the pot after about $1^{1}/_{2}$ hours. Cook for another $1/2$ hour or until meat is tender.

Taste and adjust seasoning with light soya sauce, salt and pepper if needed. Garnish with chopped parsley and serve.

MINUTE STEAK
[For 4]

Truly a name from the past, though it is still found in Singapore menus today. Actually a fried steak, it typically refers to a thin slice of meat that is cooked literally in minutes. While there are American and English versions, this one with a brown sauce is the most familiar here.

    4 thin (about 1cm thick) slices of beef, flank or skirt
    1 tbs butter
    5 shallots, peeled and chopped
    2 cups red wine
    Salt and black pepper to taste

Melt butter in a frying pan and fry chopped shallots till softened. Remove shallots. Heat up pan again and add the steaks, one at a time.

Grind salt and pepper over the meat. Press down the steak in the pan to sear it, cooking for just a minute on each side. Set aside and cook remaining steaks.

Return shallots to the pan, add red wine, bring to the boil and cook until gravy is thick and syrupy. It should take just two minutes. Spoon gravy over steaks and serve at once with lightly boiled peas and beans and thick French fries.

SAMBAL PRAWNS
[For 6]

    500 g (1 lb) medium-sized prawns
    $^1/_4$ cup vegetable oil
    2 large onions, sliced
    1 tbs chilli powder
    1 tsp salt
    $^1/_2$ tsp sugar
    3 tomatoes, quartered

Peel prawns, leaving the tails intact. De vein and set aside.

Heat oil in a wok and saute onions till soft. Wet chilli powder to make a paste. Add to wok and fry till fragrant. Add prawns and cook over high heat till pink. Season with salt and sugar and toss tomatoes in at the last minute. Serve at once with white rice.

The Hainanese version of the nonya sambal prawns became popular in their eateries, simply because there was more prawns, onions and delicious fragrant oil. Unlike the nonya version, this Chinese sambal was a stir-fried dish, quite distinct in its own right.

ROTI BABI [For 8]

Hard to find commercially in Singapore, Roti Babi is an old-time nonya speciality still offered at the Coliseum Cafe in Kuala Lumpur. Better than fried bread, that sinful British invention, a meat mixture tops the sliced bread before it is fried!

> 8 slices of stale bread
> 300 g (10 oz) minced pork or chicken
> 1 onion, finely chopped
> 1 egg
> 1 tsp salt
> Pepper
> 1 tsp corn flour

Mix minced meat together with onion, egg, salt, pepper and corn flour. Trim off crusts of bread slices, if desired.

Heat wok half full with oil. In the meantime, spread meat mixture evenly on each slice of the bread. Test if oil is hot enough by frying first a small piece of bread, the oil should sizzle.

Once oil is hot enough, carefully slide in bread, meat side down, into the oil and fry till golden brown. Turn over to fry the other side till golden brown.

Remove and drain on kitchen paper. Serve hot with this classic Hainanese dip of sliced red chillies in Worcestershire sauce.

CHICKEN MARYLAND [For 4]

It was a favourite fried chicken dish in the 1970s and nobody could believe how much there was on the plate — for not only was there a chicken chop, there was also a fried banana, corn fritters, even bacon and sometimes a sausage! As American as McDonalds, it came earlier than the burger chain and it was the thing to order if you felt very sophisticated.

4 chicken thighs, trimmed of fat and skin
Flour seasoned with 1 tsp paprika, salt and pepper
1 egg, beaten
4 rashers of bacon
4 bananas, peeled
4 tomatoes, halved

Corn Fritters:
200g (7 oz) sweet corn kernels
    (cut from the cob and cooked in salted water)
2 eggs
Fresh white breadcrumbs or flour
Salt and pepper

Dip chicken thighs into the beaten egg, then coat with seasoned flour. Heat 1 tbs butter and vegetable oil in a frying pan. When butter froths up, fry coated chicken over a gentle fire — it should take about half an hour — and turn over halfway to brown the other side. Remove from pan and leave the chicken to warm on a rack in a low oven.

Whisk the eggs, the sweetcorn and seasoning. Add enough breadcrumbs to make a thickish batter. Leave aside.

Remove most of the oil and any debris from the pan used to fry the chicken. Put in tablespoons of the corn mixture, allow to set and fry until they are puffed up and both sides are golden brown. Drain on kitchen paper and warm in the oven together with the chicken.

Now cook the other accompaniments: Fry the banana, sprinkled with a little sugar and a little butter, turning over often, until golden. Grill the bacon and tomato halves until slightly burnt in parts.

To serve: Surround each serving of fried chicken with the fried banana, the corn fritters, the bacon and the tomato halves. Traditionally, this is served with horseradish sauce, but in Singapore, we ate it unsullied or with tomato ketchup!

WORCESTERSHIRE SAUCE
Did you know that Worcestershire sauce is a nineteenth century English sauce based on oriental ingredients such as vinegar, sugar, soy sauce, molasses, tamarind, shallots, anchovies, ginger, chilli, cloves, nutmeg and cardamom?

Aside from Hainanese cooks, the Nonyas also took fervently to this *ang moh tau yu* (white man's soy sauce in Hokkien) and with sliced red chillies, it has become an essential accompaniment for dishes such as Inchee Kabin (Penang fried chicken), ikan panggang (grilled fish) as well as roti babi.

FRIED MAH MEE [For 6]

The fresh yellow noodles now known as Hokkien noodles, was called mah mee in the old days. It was offered in snack bars menus before Cantonese noodles became popular.

500g (1 lb) fresh yellow noodles
200g (7 oz) small prawns
200g (7 oz) chicken or pork
2 cups of water
6 stalks of chye sim (mustard greens)
1 tbs oil
1 tbs chopped garlic
1 tbs sliced shallots
1 tbs light soya sauce
1 tsp dark soya sauce
1 tsp cornflour made into a paste with some water
Salt and pepper to taste
1 tsp sugar

Garnishes:
Fried shallots
Spring onion
Red chilli
Fresh coriander leaves
Omelette strips, using 2 eggs

Prepare the garnishes. Break two eggs into a bowl, season with a pinch of salt and fry in a little oil in a hot pan to make an omelette. When cool, cut into thin strips. Slice spring onion and chilli thinly. Wash and cut coriander leaves into short lengths. Leave all aside.

Now ready the ingredients. Peel prawns. Reserve prawns and shells. Bring two cups of water to the boil and cook shells till they turn pink. Remove. Add pork or chicken meat to the same pot. Remove after about 10 minutes. When cool, shred meat. Reserve this stock.

Wash and cut chye sim into 5 cm lengths. Heat oil in a wok, large enough to accommodate the noodles. When hot, saute garlic and shallots till fragrant. Add prawns and shredded meat. Season with the soya sauces. Add the stock, thickened with the cornflour. Add sugar. Bring to the boil, stirring all the time.

Add the vegetables, then the loosened noodles. Mix well. Adjust seasoning if needed. Remember that Hokkien noodles come ready salted. Garnish with fried shallots, sliced spring onions and chilli, omelette strips and coriander leaves.

HAINANESE PORK CHOPS [For 6]

Unique to Singapore, you cannot find pork chops like these elsewhere. While it is European inspired, the execution is entirely Chinese, well, Hainanese actually. Again soya sauce and even tomato sauce is found in the recipe.

600 gm (1.1 lb) lean pork, sliced thickly into chops
2 tsp light soya sauce
2 tsp rice wine
$1/_2$ tsp salt
White pepper
$1/_2$ cup oil

2 eggs, beaten
4 tbs flour mixed with 1 tbs cornflour
$1/_2$ cup breadcrumbs
$1/_2$ tsp salt

1 large onion, sliced
1 cup water
$1/_2$ tsp cornflour
$1/_2$ tsp dark soya sauce
1 tbs bottled tomato sauce
$1/_2$ tsp salt
Pepper
2 tomatoes, quartered
1 cup peas

Place pork into a bowl and marinate with the light soya sauce, rice wine, salt and pepper. Leave covered in the fridge for at least an hour.

Heat half cup oil in a wok. Get ready beaten egg in a bowl, flour seasoned with salt on a plate and breadcrumbs on another plate. When oil is hot, coat pork slices first in the egg, then the flour mixture and finally the breadcrumbs. Fry coated pork till lightly browned. Remove and drain on kitchen paper. Slice when cool.

Drain off all but 2 tbs of the oil. Saute sliced onions, then the tomatoes and peas. Add the water, in which the cornflour has been rendered, then the salt, soya sauce and tomato sauce. Allow to thicken. Adjust seasoning if needed and pour over the pork chops. Serve at once.

CHOCOLATE ECLAIRS [Makes 8]

100 g (3 oz) choux pastry (see page 26)

Vanilla cream:
150 ml ($^2/_3$ cup) whipping cream
2 drops vanilla essence
10 gsm ($^1/_3$ oz) caster sugar

Chocolate icing:
50 g (approx 2 oz) plain chocolate
1 tbs butter
2-3 tbs water
100 g ($^7/_8$ cup) icing sugar

Heat the oven to 200°C. Lightly grease a large baking sheet.

Make choux pastry and while still warm, put it into piping bag fitted with a 2 cm plain nozzle. Pipe 10-cm lengths of pastry onto baking sheet, cutting off each strip with a knife dipped in warm water.

Bake for 40 minutes until puffed up and golden. Remove eclair shells from baking sheet to cool on a wire rack. Split each one lengthways in half with a sharp knife and remove any uncooked pastry within. Leave to cool completely.

Now make the vanilla cream. Whip the cream until it holds its shape, then add vanilla essence and sugar and whisk until thick but not stiff. Spoon vanilla cream into the split éclair, and cover with the tops.

To make the chocolate icing, grate chocolate into a small pan. Add butter and 1 tbs. water. Warm gently, stirring occasionally, until mixture is smooth and creamy.

Sift the icing sugar and add it a little at a time. If necessary, thin it down with 1-2 tbs water to make a coating consistency.

Spread icing over the tops of the eclairs at once, then leave to set.

MILK SHAKES [For 4]

The best milk shakes in Singapore in the 1960s could be found at Honeyland Milk Bar along Battery Road where they were so thick that you could stand a spoon in it.

2 cups milk
8 scoops vanilla ice cream

Pour milk into blender. Add half the ice-cream. Cover and blend till smooth. Scrape down the sides of the blender and add the rest of the ice-cream.

At this point, you may add the flavourings, which may be 1 banana, 1 cup of strawberries or $^1/_2$ cup chocolate, coffee or fruit syrups. Process for just three to five seconds, any longer and the ice cream will liquefy.

BANANA SPLIT [For 4-6]

Fantastical ice-cream concoctions were introduced to the Singaporean via the Magnolia milk bars that served sundaes, floats and ice-cream specialities. The Banana Split was everyone's favourite.

3-6 ripe bananas
$^1/_2$ litre each of vanilla, strawberry and chocolate ice cream
1 cup chopped walnuts
1 cup chocolate chips
$^1/_2$ cup butter
1 cup cream
$^1/_2$ cup of tinned crushed pineapple, drained
$^1/_2$ cup cream, whipped
Chocolate sprinkles
Maraschino cherries

Peel and slice bananas length-wise. Place in a flat oval ice-cream dish with a gap in between the slices. Place a scoop of each flavour of ice cream in the gap. Freeze until firm.

Melt chocolate chips with butter in a heatproof bowl in a microwave oven. Add 1 cup of cream. Stir. When cool, pour chocolate sauce over ice cream concoction. Top with chopped pineapple. Freeze until firm.

Whip extra cream, spread it over the chocolate layer, and top with nuts and chocolate sprinkles. Garnish with a cherry.

KNICKERBOCKER GLORY [For 4-6]

A very elaborate ice cream sundae of layers of ice cream, jelly, fruit and cream in a tall glass and topped with sweet sauces, nuts and whipped cream. A British treat, it was found on the menus of the Magnolia milk bars for years.

One litre vanilla ice cream
Fresh fruits, such as bananas, strawberries or raspberries
1 packet of raspberry or other fruit jelly

Chocolate sauce:
1 cup chocolate chips
$^1/_2$ cup butter
$^1/_2$ cup cream

Melba sauce:
2 cups raspberries
Juice of $^1/_2$ lemon
2 tbs caster sugar
1 tsp corn flour

Toppings:
Whipped cream
$^1/_2$ cup chopped nuts, such as peanuts or walnuts
Mint or maraschino cherries

Make the jelly according to packet instructions. Leave to set. Chop jelly into cubes.

Meanwhile, make the Melba and chocolate sauces. Put raspberries, lemon juice and sugar in a pan and heat gently until the sugar has dissolved.

Mix corn flour to a paste with a little cold water. Stir the paste into the raspberry sauce and bring to the boil. Lower the heat and simmer until the sauce thickens, stirring constantly. Leave to cool.

To make the chocolate sauce, melt chocolate chips and butter in a heatproof bowl on low heat in the microwave oven. Stir in the cream. You should end up with a glossy sauce.

Wash and cut up fresh fruits into small, bite-sized pieces.

To make up the sundae, you will need four to six tall tumblers or knickerbocker glory glasses (tall sundae glasses).

Place layers of ice cream, followed by a drizzle of Melba sauce, fruit, jelly and cream in the sundae glasses up to the very top, finishing with the cream.

Top with chocolate sauce. Sprinkle with chopped nuts, topped with fresh mint leaves and a maraschino cherry.

DURIAN

STRAWBERRY

SWEETC

THE CANTONESE BANQUET

Revolutions in dining out

IN THE EARLY TWENTIETH CENTURY, the Chinese restaurants in Singapore were all Cantonese. But as a proud Cantonese pointed out, Canton then was the culinary capital of the Guangdong region and indeed of all China. The city had more restaurants and culinary inventions than any other city in China.

The early immigrants to Singapore were also mostly Southern Chinese who included the Cantonese, of course, and also the Hokkiens and Teochews. And they brought with them their special skills, which in the case of the Cantonese, was cooking. No wonder then that Cantonese food became the best-known Chinese food in Singapore. Oldsters remember that if they were invited to a banquet in those days, it would be at the Cantonese restaurants, and most likely, it would be at Wing Choon Yeun.

Established in 1929, it was the restaurant to go to for weddings, birthdays and yes, baby's first-month celebrations. Still operating today, its executive chairman, Mr. Ho Hun Cheong, even remembers the restaurant hosting introduction dinners, where prospective young couples were brought together to meet. Run by his father, it used to operate out of an old colonial bungalow in Great World Amusement Park and later branched out to New Bridge Road where it was re-named Spring Court and finally found its way to Upper East Coast Road after the Chinatown branch closed down.

The plush Cathay Restaurant, housed on the fourth floor of the first skyscraper in Singapore, brought in the first Hongkong chefs — and it was a revolution.

The other old-time name is Tai Tong, which has re-emerged under its hanyu pinyin name, Da Dong, and is now located at Smith Street, two streets away from its original site. The father of its director and culinary consultant, Mr Leong Siew Kwai started the original restaurant in Mosque Street in 1928, but de-registered it, following re-development of the site in 1995, losing its age-old brand name to someone else in the process. The two restaurants were among the only eight or so Chinese restaurants operating then, all Cantonese. They include long-gone names such as Airview Restaurant, Nam Tien, New Era or Sun Kee Yeun and Empress Restaurant.

After the war in 1948, the plush Cathay Restaurant re-opened with a grand dinner. To this restaurant, housed on the fourth floor of Cathay Building, the first skyscraper in Singapore, would go the distinction of bringing in the first Hongkong chefs here — and it was a revolution. Hongkong cooking was more refined and beautifully presented unlike the gutsy, full-flavoured family style of local Cantonese food. This created a continuing habit of looking towards Hongkong for culinary inspiration.

However, Cantonese chefs from Singapore have left an impressive legacy of food that includes creative new dishes such as the Lunar New Year Raw Fish Salad, which has become a Singapore eating tradition. After World War Two, Ng Chew Kee started his eponymous restaurant in Chinatown and introduced a version of the salad which had 36 ingredients tossed with slices of paper-thin Ikan Parang. A group of Cantonese chefs continued to popularise eating the salad so that today, it is ordered as a matter of course

during Chinese New Year. The chefs were Tham Yui Kai, Sin Leong, Hooi Kok Wai and Lau Yeok Pui, who also worked hard to popularise Cantonese cuisine with cookbooks and cooking lessons. A legion of women learnt how to steam chicken with ham, make yam baskets and fry crisp whole chickens — all banquet dishes — under their instruction.

In the past, people ate in restaurants to celebrate important occasions so the dishes offered on the menus were special. While a whole steamed fish may be the centrepiece, chicken was the luxury meat, hence the predominance of chicken dishes on the banquet table. Such a special meal would begin and end with a soup, with the piece de resistance being a whole suckling pig.

Some of these old-time dishes are still served at Cantonese restaurants. At Spring Court, you will find the old-fashioned thick sharks' fin soup, brimming with fresh crabmeat, being served. Their suckling pigs are still roasted over an open fire like in the old days. And customers visiting the new Da Dong will find old favourites such as the tai pau (or giant bao) of the old days, bursting with chicken, sausage, egg and prawns and the lesser known, but equally traditional, Whampoa noodles fried with scrambled egg and prawns.

Other well-known Cantonese dishes actually have a shorter history. A closer look at so-called classics such as Chinese beefsteak and even sweet and sour pork will find imported ingredients such as HP sauce, mayonnaise and tomato sauce in the recipes as Western ingredients made inrouads into erstwhile traditional recipes. Today, they are indistinguishable from the classic seasonings of ginger and spring onion, black bean and chilli that still flavour the dishes today. They have become the new classics of Cantonese eating.

WINTER MELON SOUP [For 4-6]

Try to obtain Chinese ham for this soup for its distinctive flavour makes this clear, clean soup. Serving it in the whole melon makes for a stunning presentation.

1 whole winter melon, about 4 kg
2 cups chicken stock
4 Chinese dried black mushrooms
2-3 slices ginger
$^1/_4$ cup boneless chicken meat, diced
$^1/_4$ cup Chinese ham, diced
$^1/_4$ cup small shrimp, peeled
$^1/_4$ cup diced carrots
Light soya sauce, salt and pepper to taste

Soak dried mushrooms in 1 cup hot water. When softened, cut off the tough end of the stalk, and cut mushrooms into quarters. Reserve soaking water. Cut off and reserve the top of the winter melon, remove seeds and wash out the cavity.

Place mushrooms, ginger, chicken, ham, shrimp and carrots in the cavity. Fill with chicken stock and mushroom soaking water, taking care not to include the sediment. Season to taste. Cover with the top of the melon.

Place the whole melon on a deep plate and stand it in a wok, half filled with water. Cover wok and steam melon for 1 hour.

To serve, bring the whole melon to the table, Use a soup ladle to scoop out some of the pulp as you serve the soup.

CHICKEN WITH CORN SOUP [For 4-6]

This soup is thickened with corn kernels and beaten egg. While the recipe relies mainly on the sweetness of corn and a good stock, the addition of crabmeat, dried scallops or Chinese ham would enrich it further.

1 cup sweet corn kernels from a can or fresh
4 cups chicken stock
2 slices fresh ginger
50 g (approx 2 oz) minced chicken,
    seasoned with light soya sauce
2 tbs corn flour
$^1/_4$ cup water
1 egg, beaten
1 stalk spring onion, chopped
White pepper

Mash drained corn kernels in a mortar or chop in a food processor to break it up. Add mashed corn kernels to a pot together with chicken stock and ginger. Bring to boil, reduce heat, cover and simmer for 5 minutes. Discard ginger slices. Add minced chicken, stirring to break it up.

Combine corn flour and $^1/_4$ cup water; stir into pot, stirring constantly, until mixture is slightly thickened. Gradually pour egg into boiling soup and stir it a few times in one direction. Remove from heat; add spring onions and soy sauce. Serve immediately seasoned with a shake of white pepper.

SHARK'S FIN SOUP [For 6-8]

This is the old-time thickened soup we loved long before the Hongkong clear version using superior fins and stock became popular. Here, a chicken stock, flavoured with ham and scallops and the addition of fresh crabmeat truly makes the dish and of course, a touch of black Chinese vinegar lifts the flavours.

100 g (approx 3 oz) dried shark's fins
Meat from 2 crabs or 2 cups fresh crabmeat
2-4 slices Chinese ham, cut into strips
10 dried scallops
1 stalk spring onion
1 ginger slice
6 cups chicken stock
1 tbs Chinese wine or sherry
1 tbs salt
2 tbs corn flour
White pepper

Soak dried fins in water for at least 12 hours or overnight in the fridge. Drain. Place softened fins in the top tier of a double-boiler. Add 2 cups of chicken stock and steam for three hours or until soft. Drain, reserve fins and stock. Omit this step if you are using pre-softened fins.

In the meantime, if using fresh crab, place crabs in the freezer to send them to sleep, then steam the crabs for about eight minutes. Leave to cool covered for 10 minutes. Pry off the shell, the hard bits in the middle and the feathery gills. Cut the body into four. Extract the flesh, using nutcracker, skewers and a pair of scissors. Reserve meat.

Steam dried scallop, ham, ginger and spring onion with a cup of water in another double-boiler for 1 hour. Remove spring onion and ginger. Reserve scallops, which should be soft enough to shred, ham and stock.

To assemble the soup, boil the rest of the chicken stock, the wine and reserved stocks in a pot. Add the softened fins and cook for 15 minutes or so. Thicken with corn flour made first into a paste with a little water. Stir continuously over medium heat till the soup thickens. Season with salt and pepper

Just before serving, stir in crabmeat, scallops and ham. Serve hot with Chinese red vinegar on the side.

LOBSTER WITH FRUIT SALAD

[For 10, as part of a meal]

This lobster salad is still served in Spring Court, which touts the dish as one of its old-time dishes. The use of mayonnaise, peas and in the past, even tinned mixed fruit, marks it as one with Asian American influence.

1 lobster (aprox. 800 g, 1.5 lb), already cooked or live
$1/_2$ cup sweet green peas
1 carrot, diced
1 apple, peeled and diced
$1/_2$ cup mayonnaise
1 tbs chilli sauce
Juice from $1/_2$ a lemon
$1/_4$ tsp salt
Pepper to taste
Lettuce as garnish

If live, place lobster in the freezer for a couple of hours to send it to sleep. Boil a pot of water and cook lobster for about eight minutes or till it turns red. Leave it to cool in the pot for 10 minutes.

Pry off the shell, saving the head and tail. Remove lobster meat with a small sharp knife and dice. Leave aside.

Lightly boil the peas, dice the apple and carrot and place in a bowl together with the lobster meat. Mix well with the mayonnaise, chilli sauce, lemon juice, salt and pepper.

To assemble, line a plate with lettuce leaves. Place dressed lobster meat mixture in a mound in the middle and place lobster head and tail at either end of the plate to reassemble the crustacean. Serve cold.

SHRIMP TOAST [Makes 32]

8 slices day-old white bread
400 g (12 oz) fresh shrimp
$1/_2$ medium onion, chopped
1 tsp ginger, finely chopped
$1/_2$ tsp salt
White pepper
1 egg, lightly beaten
1 tbs corn flour
A few drops sesame oil
1 tsp sherry

Trim bread of crusts. Cut each slice into four squares, making 32 in all. Peel shrimp, de-vein and chop roughly. Add onion to shrimp and mince until fine. Add ginger, corn flour, egg, salt, white pepper, sherry and sesame oil. Mix well, throwing mixture against the side of basin to obtain a firmer texture.

Place a mound of shrimp mixture on a bread square, using wet fingers to neaten. Repeat for the rest of the squares.

Heat a wok half filled with oil. Test temperature by tossing a piece of bread into the oil, It should sizzle. Carefully slide bread pieces into the wok, a few at a time, shrimp side down. Deep-fry until golden, about 2 minutes, then turn and fry the other side for one minute. Drain on paper towels. Serve hot.

FU YONG HAI [For 4-6]

A crabmeat and shark's fin omelette, it can be found in old-time Cantonese restaurants everywhere in the world.

4 eggs
$1/_2$ tsp sugar
1 tsp dry sherry
$1/_2$ tsp salt
White pepper
1 tbs corn flour
2 tbs water
2 tbs vegetable oil
2 ginger slices
1 cup cleaned crabmeat, available from supermarkets
1 cup prepared shark's fins, available from supermarkets
1 cup fresh bean sprouts
1 tsp soya sauce
A few drops of sesame oil
1 stalk spring onion, chopped

Beat eggs together in medium bowl with sugar, sherry, salt and pepper. Add water to corn flour to make into a paste and stir into beaten egg mixture. Leave aside.

Heat oil in large non-stick fry pan over medium-high heat. Fry ginger slices. After a few minutes, discard ginger. Saute bean sprouts, crabmeat and shark's fins in this flavoured oil. Season with light soya sauce and a few drops of sesame oil.

Pour beaten egg over crabmeat mixture and cook without stirring till egg is set. Garnish with spring onions, stir lightly and serve immediately.

No sesame seeds on this savoury snack - that was to come later. This one - just minced fresh prawn atop a bread square, was an essential appetiser at any Chinese banquet and most likely has western roots.

HAR LOK [For 6]

This is caramalised prawns, which are as delicious as they are quick to cook. They typify the kind of cooking for which the Cantonese chefs are famed for, the freshest ingredients flavoured with sauce and cooked in a snap!

500 g (1 lb) fresh large prawns, shells kept on
1 tsp salt
Vegetable oil for deep frying
4 cloves garlic, chopped
1 thumb-length ginger, chopped
4 stalks spring onion, chopped

Sauce:
1 tsp corn flour
2 tbs light soya sauce
2 tsp sugar
1 tbs rice wine or dry sherry
1 tbs tomato ketchup

Wash prawns well and trim whiskers and legs. Pat dry with paper towels. Put into a large bowl, sprinkle with salt and mix well. Let stand for about 20 minutes.

Prepare the sauce in the meantime by mixing together corn flour, light soya sauce, sugar, sherry or wine and ketchup in a bowl. Leave aside.

Half fill a wok with oil. Heat till smoking hot or till a small piece of bread sizzles when tossed into the oil. The right temperature is important because you want to sear the prawns. Tip all the prawns into the oil, moving them gently with long chopsticks for about 1 minute.

Turn off the heat, remove prawns immediately using a slotted spoon and drain on paper towels.

Empty all but 2 or 3 tablespoons of oil in the wok. Reheat oil until smoking hot. Saute chopped garlic and ginger till fragrant, then return prawns to the wok. Pour sauce over, tossing prawns until most of the sauce has been absorbed. Add spring onion and serve immediately.

PRAWN FRITTERS [For 4-6]

Where can you find prawn fritters now? It is an enticing dish, with the crunch of crisp batter giving way to the sweet flesh of shrimp. Nowadays, the prawns found in a Chinese banquet are more often served steamed, following Hongkong fashion. Battered prawns, however, are definately Singaporean, dipped in Lingam's chillie sauce.

10 medium prawns, peeled and de-veined, tails left on
$^1/_2$ tsp salt
$^1/_2$ tsp sugar
Pepper
3 tsp corn flour

Batter:
$1^1/_2$ cups self-raising flour
$^1/_2$ tsp salt
Pepper
$1^1/_2$ cups water
1 egg white, beaten
1 tbs oil
Oil for deep-frying

Rub a mixture of salt, pepper, sugar and corn flour into prawns. Leave for 15 minutes. To make batter, sift flour into bowl, then add in salt and pepper. Gradually add water to make a smooth and slightly thick batter. Leave to stand for half an hour. Beat in oil and fold in beaten egg white.

Heat oil in deep fryer, dip prawns in batter and fry till golden. Drain and serve immediately with chilli sauce.

CHINESE FRIED CHICKEN [For 10 as part of a meal]

This is the old-fashioned Cantonese roast chicken, which is marinated, hung out to dry and then fried twice to produce that crisp skin. Here the process is simplified and brought up to date by first par-roasting the bird in a low oven.

1 chicken, approximately $1^1/_2$ kg (3 lb)
1 tsp five-spice powder
1 tbs salt
2 tbs sherry or rice wine
1 stalk spring onion
1 ginger slice

Rinse and dry the chicken inside and out and rub it with five-spice powder and salt. Place spring onion and ginger into the cavity.

Brush chicken with sherry or rice wine. Par-roast bird for half an hour at 150˚C.

Fill the wok half full of oil and heat till smoking hot. Put in the chicken, breast side down, and reduce heat to low. Fry for 10 minutes and then fry the other side for another four to five minutes. Be sure to baste the chicken both inside and out with the oil. Remove, drain the chicken and let it cool slightly.

Turn up heat again and return the chicken to the wok to fry until the skin is crisp and golden.

Remove and drain chicken on kitchen towels. Remove the spring onion and ginger. Cut chicken into pieces and serve with spiced salt (that is, salt mixed with five spice powder).

STEAMED CHICKEN WITH HAM
[Four 10 as part of meal]

A classic Cantonese chicken dish, which is seldom found on menus except at old restaurants such as Spring Court and Da Dong. It makes for an impressive banquet dish, with chicken pieces reassembled for form a whole chicken, resting on a bed of dark greens.

1 chicken, approximately $1^1/_2$ kg (3 lb)
1 tbs salt
1 stalk spring onion
1 ginger slices
100 g (approx 3 oz) ham
300 g (approx 9 oz) kai lan (Chinese kale), parboiled
1 cup of chicken stock
1 tsp light soya sauce
1 tbs rice wine
1 tsp sugar
1 tsp corn flour

Rub salt all over chicken, place spring onion and ginger in chicken cavity and steam bird for 20 minutes. When cool, discard spring onion and ginger, de-bone chicken and chop into small pieces.

Cut ham into pieces the same-size as the chicken. Place chicken and ham alternately on a plate. Decorate with Chinese kale. Place plate on a stand in a wok half filled with water and steam, covered, for 10 minutes.

In the meantime, combine stock, light soya sauce, wine, sugar and corn flour, in a pot. Cook over a medium fire stirring continuously until sauce is thickened. Pour sauce over the chicken just before serving.

CHICKEN WITH CASHEWS

[For 6]

The Cantonese chef is expert at stir-frying, which calls for a well-heated wok, correct temperature and quick deft action. Pre-mix all the sauces before you start cooking.

300 g (approx 9 oz) boneless chicken, cut into cubes
$^1/_4$ cup peanut oil
$^2/_3$ cup raw cashews or roasted cashews
1 thumb-length ginger, sliced
15 snow peas

Marinade:
1 tsp light soya sauce
1 tsp corn flour
1 tsp rice wine or dry sherry
$^1/_2$ tsp sugar

Sauce:
$^1/_4$ cup chicken stock or water
1 tsp light soya sauce
1 tsp corn flour
1 tsp rice wine or dry sherry
$^1/_2$ tsp sugar

Mix chicken cubes thoroughly in marinade of light soya sauce, corn flour, rice wine and sugar. Leave for 15 minutes or so. String snow peas.

Combine sauce ingredients — stock, light soya sauce, corn flour, rice wine and sugar in a bowl. Mix well and set aside.

Heat oil in a wok over medium heat and fry the cashews for about 2 minutes until golden. Use a slotted spoon to remove the nuts. Set aside. Omit this step if you use roasted cashews.

Remove all but 2 tbs of the oil. Add the ginger and fry till fragrant. Add chicken and snow peas. Cook, adding a splash of water to moisten. After a few minutes, add sauce, stirring constantly until thickened.

Return cashews to the wok. Stir well. Serve chicken with hot white rice.

Note: You can use walnuts instead of cashews and substitute the snow peas with green peppers.

Union Farm 'chee pow kai' started business in 1964 and still operates in a farmyard setting.

PAPER-WRAPPED CHICKEN

[Makes 20 parcels]

One restaurant in Singapore, Union Farm, single-handedly popularised this dish in Singapore. Originally a chicken farm, it has become a full-time restaurant still serving paper-wrapped chicken decades later. Instead of chicken, you could substitute fish or prawns in the same marinade.

1 kg (2 lb) chicken parts

Marinade:
2 tbs light soya sauce
1 stalk spring onion, chopped
1 tsp salt
2 tbs sherry or rice wine
1 tsp sugar
Thick greaseproof paper
Ginger root enough for 20 slices
2 stalks spring onion, cut into 5-cm lengths

Make up marinade and use it to marinate chicken pieces overnight covered or for at least an hour in the fridge. Cut 20 pieces of thick greaseproof paper, each about 10 cms square.

Place 1 or 2 pieces of marinated chicken meat and a length of spring onion and a ginger slice in the centre of the square. Wrap it envelope-style, inserting the flap into the packet. Do not overfill to prevent undercooking of the meat.

Heat a wok half full of oil and when smoking hot, fry 2-3 parcels at a time for about 3 minutes each time, allowing the oil to heat up again before adding more. Take care not to overcrowd the pan so that the temperature of the oil is not lowered.

When parcels are browned, remove from pan and drain on kitchen towels. Serve hot without unwrapping, but do offer a finger bowl for those greasy fingers.

CHINESE BEEF STEAK

[For 10 as part of meal]

Meat in Chinese cuisine would be sliced thinly before cooking. Here, slices of beef are marinated in a mix of familiar bottled sauces before it is flash-fried Chinese fashion.

500 g (1 lb) sirloin steak
Vegetable oil for deep-frying
Lettuce, optional

Marinade:
2 slices ginger, finely chopped
1 tbs dry sherry
1 tbs light soya sauce
A few drops of sesame oil
White pepper

Sauce:
1 tbs tomato ketchup
1 tbs Worcestershire sauce
1 tbs sugar
1 tsp light soya sauce
1 tbs corn flour
1 tsp salt
$1/_2$ cup water

Combine marinade ingredients. Slice beef into 1-cm thick pieces and marinate for at least half an hour.

Heat 2 tbs oil in a wok till smoking hot. Stir-fry marinated beef for about 30 seconds. Do not worry if they are not completely cooked. Remove and set aside.

In the same wok, heat blended sauce ingredients, stirring until sauce thickens. Return beef slices to the wok. Toss well to coat beef with the sauce and serve immediately on bed of fresh lettuce, if liked.

CANTONESE FRIED RICE

[For 10 as part of a meal]

Often the final course before the soup, this dish is meant to fill those empty spaces still left after sitting down to a 10-course meal. This is the traditional recipe but today, there are many variations of fried rice - the most popular of which must be fried rice with salted fish. The Malay food stalls took this further and substituted crunchy ikan bilis for the salted fish and produced another hit!

2 tbs vegetable oil
3 cloves garlic, chopped
Thumb-length ginger, chopped
1 medium onion, chopped
$1/_2$ cup ham, diced
$1/_2$ cup char siew (barbecued pork), diced
$1/_2$ cup small shrimps, peeled
1 cup green peas
1 tbs light soya sauce
6 cups cooked rice
2 eggs, beaten
1 stalk spring onion, chopped
1 tsp salt
Pepper to taste
Lettuce, optional
Pickled green chillies

Heat oil in a wok. Saute garlic and ginger till fragrant. Add onions, ham, char siew and shrimp. Stir well before adding the peas. Season with light soya sauce.

Now add the rice. Season with salt and pepper. Toss continuously to ensure that every grain of rice is coated with the flavoured oil and the ingredients are well mixed.

Make a well in the middle of the rice. Heat a tsp. of oil in this space and pour in the beaten eggs. Allow to set, then cover with the rice to steam cook. After a few minutes, toss thoroughly again. Top with spring onion and serve immediately.

If liked, serve fried rice on a fresh lettuce leaf to cut through the richness. Top with pickled green chillies.

RAW FISH SALAD

[For 10]

300 g (approx 9 oz) fresh ikan parang (wolf herring)

Dressing:
$1/_2$ cup bottled plum sauce
4-5 tbs vegetable oil
Juice from 4 limes or to taste
Salt and pepper to taste
$1/_4$ tsp five-spice powder

Salad:
2 carrots, shredded
2 Chinese radish, shredded
2 pomelo segments, skin removed and sacs separated

Toppings:
2 tbs pickled red ginger strips
2 tbs fresh ginger strips
4 pickled leeks, shredded
1 tbs candied winter melon, shredded, optional
1 tbs candied orange peel, shredded, optional

Garnishes:
4 red chillies, cut into strips
2 stalks Chinese celery,
    leaves plucked and stems cut into short lengths
2 daun limau purut (kaffir lime leaves), finely shredded
$1/_2$ cup peanuts, chopped
A scattering of white sesame seeds
1 cup crisp wheat crackers
    (from Chinatown confectioneries)

The day before: Prepare the toppings, garnishes and dressing. Basically everything needs to be shredded finely. Store separately in the fridge till needed. Place dressing ingredients in a large screwtop jar and shake vigorously till all is combined. Store in fridge till needed.

The day itself: Buy the fish, store in the freezer till semi-frozen to make handling easier and slice thinly. Leave in fridge till needed.

Using a hand shredder, shred carrot and radish into thin strips. Peel the pomelo segments and separate the sacs.

To assemble: Place shredded vegetables on a large plate. Top with the pickled and candied ingredients. Arrange fish on top. Garnish with the chillies, herbs and crunchies. Pour on the dressing just before everyone tosses the salad.

A Singapore invention. This dish calls for a mountain of shredded vegetables but offers diners the convenience of ready-mixed sauce. The salad is then tossed by the whole table to demonstrate togetherness, actually a marketing strategy that capitalised on the well-entrenched practice of families sharing at least one meal during Chinese New Year. Today, the wolf herring is often substituted with salmon and there are even Japanese and Thai versions of the dish!

SWEET AND SOUR PORK
[For 4-6]

This is a dish that has found a legion of fans round the world who loved its sweet-sour taste. Today, the dish is still popular but the battered pork is served separately from the sauce so that its crisp crunch remains.

500 g (1 lb) lean pork, cut into bite-size pieces
Vegetable oil for frying
1 onion, quartered
1 carrot, sliced diagonally
1 cucumber, sliced diagonally

Batter:
2 eggs, well-beaten
$^3/_4$ cup cold water
1 cup flour
1 tsp salt
Pepper to taste

Sauce:
4 tbs tomato sauce
3 tbs sugar
4 tbs sherry
1 tbs light soy sauce
3 tbs white vinegar
2 tbs corn flour

Blend well batter ingredients in a large bowl. Leave aside for an hour. Combine sauce ingredients, taste to adjust seasoning and leave aside.

Fill wok half full with oil and heat till smoking. Dip pork pieces into batter a few pieces at a time. Deep-fry till golden, about five minutes. Drain on kitchen towels and keep warm in a low oven.

Remove all but 2 tbs of oil from the wok. Stir-fry onions and carrots quickly. Add sauce to the wok, stirring all the while till sauce thickens. Finally add the cucumbers. Place battered pork on a serving dish, pour over sauce and serve immediately.

BEEF HOR FUN [For 8-10]

500 g (1 lb) dried or fresh hor fun (flat rice noodles)
300 g (approx 9 oz) flank steak, sliced thinly

Marinade:
1 tsp light soya sauce
1 tsp sesame oil
1 tsp rice wine

250 g ($^1/_2$ lb) kai lan (Chinese kale), lightly boiled
4 tbs peanut oil
1 clove garlic, chopped
4 shallots, sliced thinly
1 thumb-length ginger, chopped

Sauce:
2 cups stock or water
1 tbs light soy sauce
1 tbs oyster sauce
1 tbs rice wine
1 tsp salt
1 tsp sesame oil
1 tbs sugar
1 tbs corn flour

The popularity of this dish is demonstrated by the number of places where you can eat it - in food stalls, restaurants and lots of club cafes. The secret to this dish is making sure you have ample gravy to drench the noodles with.

Soak dried noodles in cold water till softened. Bring a pot of water with a little oil to boil and cook drained noodles. It takes just minutes. Break off a strand to test if noodles are cooked. Place drained noodles on a plate. Omit this step if using fresh noodles.

Slice steak thinly across grain and cut each slice again in half if you want small pieces. Marinate in light soya sauce, sesame oil and rice wine. Leave to stand at least 15 minutes.

Heat oil in a wok large enough for the noodles. Saute garlic, shallots and ginger till fragrant. Add beef slices and stir-fry briskly for a few minutes. Do not worry if they are half cooked. Remove.

Mix sauce ingredients in a bowl, stirring well. Pour sauce into hot wok and allow to thicken, stirring continuously. Return beef to the wok. Add green vegetables and pour sauce over noodles on the plate. Serve immediately with a dip of pickled green chillies and light soya sauce on the side.

PRAWNS AND VEGETABLES IN A YAM BASKET

[For 10 as part of a meal]

Contrasting texture, colour and appearance are found in this impressive dish which also calls for good technique in deep frying. In a variation, mashed yam is formed into a ring then deep fried, before filling it with sautéed vegetables. Both dishes demand extensive preparation, the mark of a banquet dish!

1 yam, about 500 gsm (1 lb)
3 tbs corn flour
4 cups oil for deep-frying

Filling:
12 fresh prawns, shelled and de-veined
1 piece canned bamboo shoot, sliced diagonally
1 carrot, sliced diagonally
10 snow peas, remove strings
2 tbs peanut oil
3 slices ginger, chopped
1 clove garlic, chopped
$1/2$ cup chicken stock or water
1 tbs rice wine or sherry
$1/2$ tsp sugar
1 pinch salt
Pepper
2 tsp light soya sauce
1 tbs corn flour
2 cups shredded lettuce

The yam basket can be made in advance. Peel, then cut yam into long strips. Rinse strips in cold water and soak for half hour in cold salted water. Drain. Rub corn flour on wet yam strips.

Half fill wok with oil and heat. Test heat with a yam strip — it should brown in 30 seconds. Arrange strips one by one to make a nest in a Chinese metal strainer (which has an upright bamboo handle for ease of handling) or similar strainer. Press into position with another strainer. Immerse in oil and deep-fry until basket is golden (about 8 minutes). Remove from oil, remove top strainer and reserve basket till time to serve.

When ready to serve, heat oil again. Deep-fry basket in strainer again until crisp. Drain on kitchen paper before placing basket on bed of lettuce.

Now cook the filling. Heat oil in wok. Saute ginger and garlic. Add prawns, bamboo shoot and carrot; stir-fry 1 minute. Add snow peas, salt, sugar, pepper, rice wine and light soya sauce. Toss well. Transfer prawn mixture to yam basket. Serve hot.

To ring in a change: Substitute prawns with nuts or scallops and keep vegetables to a red-yellow or all-green colour scheme.

FRUIT WITH ALMOND JELLY

[For 10]

While it looks like soya bean curd, it is actually jelly, made with soya milk here so there is more of the bean flavour. Traditionally, Chinese fruit is used but there are places which have resorted to adding tinned mixed fruit instead.

2 tbs unflavoured gelatine powder
1 cup water
2 cups soya milk
$1/2$ cup sugar
A few drops almond essence
Tinned longans, lychees and loquats

Put water in a pot and sprinkle in gelatine powder. Heat, stirring till gelatine powder dissolves. Add sugar and soya milk to the pot and stir well.

Add almond essence and pour jelly mixture into a flat dish to set in the refrigerator.

Combine tinned fruit and its syrup in a large glass bowl. Cut jelly into diamond shapes and add to the bowl. If liked decorate with maraschino cherries.

To ring in a change: Use fresh lychees and longans marinated in a lime-scented syrup.

STREET FOOD

The proof of loyal customers

GIVE THAT PLATE OF CHAR KWAY TEOW proper respect when you next
eat it. It is more than 70 years old. Honest. My 85-year-old aunt remembers eating it at Koek Road in her girlhood as she did the dishes of satay babi celop, boiled satay, and kwan chiang, Chinese boiled sausage.

For those who do not know, Koek Road was located just off Orchard Road, next to where Centrepoint Shopping Centre now stands. But it was not just a road. The name reeks of nostalgia for it was the place to eat at for many years. Together with Koek Lane, which branched off the main thoroughfare, this was where the action was most Saturday nights.

People would visit it week after week for goreng pisang, ice kachang, Hainanese pork satay and of course, those dishes mentioned above which were incidentally served in a rather dark and grimy coffee shop. But no one noticed the dirt in those days. Instead they remembered the thick aromatic stock of the gu bak kway teow, beef noodle soup, the lush richness of the oyster omelette and the simple tastes of char siu fan, actually boiled and coloured, and not barbecued, pork on rice, that was almost austere compared with the Hongkong versions that were to hit Singapore later.

Another old-time food haunt was Hock Lam Street, also a nondescript street, this time off North Bridge Road. It had just two main coffee shops but its fame spread far and wide on the island. It was an afternoon sort of place, mainly due to its location right in the shopping heart of the city as North Bridge Road and High Street then were in the 1950s and 1960s. Office workers and shoppers would throng there to eat sek bak, soya sauced braised pork and innards, hor pau, stuffed soya bean cake, and beef noodle soup. It was also the place where the now common Hakka bouncy beef balls were introduced to an enthusiastic public who loved them and their garlicky chilli sauce.

> *The food calls were distinctive – you could not mistake the nasal cry of the loh kai yik man for the gutteral calls of the ap bak (braised duck) man; nor the clacking of bamboo clappers of the noodle man....*

But even before these food places came about, Singapore already had its street food, proffered by roving hawkers, among them those who used to follow the wayang troupes on its rounds. Certain foods were associated with these wayang stalls - dessert soups such as cheng tng, made from longans and other things, green and red bean soups and Chinese cold cuts - kwan chiang (a pink pork sausage), ngo hiang (a five-spiced pork sausage) and a clutch of deep-fried tidbits eaten with chilli and a shocking pink sauce!

Less organised would be the independent hawker who would meander among neighbourhoods, balancing two large baskets of food from a pole carried on his shoulders. The legendary loh kai yik (braised chicken wings) hawker took this a step further. He was so fat that he hired a long-suffering assistant to pedal him around in a three-wheeled tricycle, with his pot of braised goodness in front of him. Other equally enterprising roving hawkers worked out a system of food delivery whereby flat-dwellers would lower baskets whenever they heard the food calls, and in this way, exchange cash for food, which was

Street food of old, sold from carts, foldable stands and baskets on poles were moveable feasts.

then carefully hoisted back up to the flats. The food calls were distinctive – you could not mistake the nasal cry of the loh kai yik man for the gutteral calls of the ap bak (braised duck) man; nor the clacking of bamboo clappers of the noodle man for the mee goreng man's insistent clanging of frying implement against wok.

Not all street hawkers would roam around calling out their wares however, some would station themselves at specific roads given over to the selling of a food speciality. The old satay club was a collection of stalls gathered around a bus depot at Beach Road. There, people would sit at low stools and dip their sticks of grilled meat into common pots of gravy! The satay man would then charge only for the sticks of satay consumed, even if he had placed before you more than that number. Similarly, Waterloo Street was famed for its Indian rojak, Hokkien Street, for Hokkien mee and Chin Swee Road, for fish-head beehoon. The latter two streets even offered al fresco dining late into the night.

Of course, the satay club and the Indian rojak stalls at Waterloo Street do not exist anymore, even if the dishes can still be eaten at other places decades later, while the Hokkien mee stalls have relocated to a multi-storeyed food centre within the same area. Only the fish-head beehoon seems to have enjoyed a lively resurgence with shops now offering their version of the creamy fish soup.

Today, the true street hawkers are no more. In the 80s, they were gathered into modern food centres with electricity and piped water supply, ensuring that their crockery and implements were washed properly at least, before the age of disposable crockery. What we loosely call street food has become a lot more sophisticated even outside the food centres, thanks mainly to the emergence of zhi char, cooked food stalls located at coffee shops. At these humble places, where you can order even 10-course banquets depending on the ingredients on offer, possibly the most innovative of Singapore cooking is on show as the stalls compete with one other to titillate the customer with yet more exciting dishes. From such places have come out relatively new Singapore gems such as hot plate tofu and butter prawns, which may or may not last the test of time as the other street foods definitely have.

KON LO MEEN [For 8]

8 bundles fresh egg noodles
300 g (approx 9 oz) chye sim (flowering Chinese cabbage)
300 g (approx 9 oz) char siew (roast pork), sliced
16-24 wontons (pork dumplings)
8 cups of fresh or canned chicken stock

Sauce (for each serving):
1 tbs bottled chilli sauce
1 tsp oyster sauce
1 tbs light soya sauce
A few drops sesame oil
1 tbs vegetable oil

Bring chicken stock to the boil and cook wontons till they float. Remove and set aside.

Boil another pot of water and scald noodles for a minute, using chopsticks to swirl noodles around. Remove, using a wire ladle and dunk noodles into a basin of cold water for a minute to stop the cooking process and return to the boiling water for a final minute. Drain and place on plate. Repeat for the other bundles of noodles.

Scald greens in the same pot of water for a couple of minutes and drain. Reserve for use later.

Mix together ingredients for the sauce, add a few tablespoons of stock to moisten, if needed, and toss cooked noodles in it one portion at a time. Top with roasted pork, dumplings and boiled greens. Serve immediately with a bowl of soup on the side.

Note: Wontons can now be bought frozen in supermarkets.

SATAY CELUP [For 5-7]

100 g (approx 3 oz) lean pork, sliced
100 g (approx 3 oz) cockles
100 g (approx 3 oz) prawns, peeled
100 g (approx 3 oz) pork liver, sliced
1 ju her (cured cuttlefish), sliced
1 cucumber
3-4 slices pineapple
5 slices of bread

Spice paste:
10 shallots, peeled
2 cloves garlic
8 dried chillies, soaked and de-seeded
2 stalks lemon grass, use white part only
1 tsp belacan (shrimp paste)
2 slices lengkwas (galangal)
5 buah keras (candlenuts)

4 cups unsalted roasted peanuts, ground
2 tbs salt
4 tbs sugar or to taste
4 cups water

Slice pork and thread on to bamboo skewers. Do the same for the other raw foods. Cut cucumber and pineapple into chunks and bread into squares. Process ingredients for spice paste in a food chopper.

Heat 2 tbs oil in a pot and sauté spice paste over a slow fire till fragrant. Add ground peanut and water, stirring while it is being added. Bring to the boil, season with salt and sugar. Taste to adjust seasoning.

Bring a small pot of water, deep enough to cook the skewered foods, to boil. Stir in half a cup of peanut gravy to the pot. Dip skewered foods into this pot to cook, according to desired doneness.

Serve skewers of cooked food, together with cucumber and pineapple, a dip of peanut gravy and bread on the side.

A marriage of Chinese steamboat and Malay satay. The skewered meats, however, are boiled instead of grilled, though the sauce is still peanut-based. The name remains enduringly Malay, even if the purveyors of the dish throughout the Malay peninsula are Chinese.

In Singapore, the most famous of such stalls was found at Koek Road, the precursor to the Orchard Road car park hawker stalls, now found at the Newton food centre. As in steamboat, you cook the skewered foods in a pot of stock placed over a brazier in the centre of the table and dip it in peanut sauce, but unusually, eat it with bread.

HOR PAU [For 8-10]

One of the earliest stalls selling sek bak (stewed meat) was again found in Hock Lam Street. The stall sold all parts of a pig, braised in soya sauces and eaten with a delectable chilli dip that had the crunch of fresh onion and green chilli. This stuffed soya cake, a variation, was filled with all that was on offer in the stall.

300 g (approx 9 oz) belly pork
1 tbs oil
2 cloves garlic, smashed
1 tbs sugar
2 tbs dark soya sauce
1 tbs light soya sauce
2 cups water
4 hard-boiled eggs
8 large-sized firm soya bean cakes
$^1/_2$ cup oil
1 cucumber
2 fried fish cakes, from wet markets
2 spiced flour rolls, from yong taufu stalls in wet markets
4 squids, left whole
1 bunch coriander leaves, chopped

Sauce:
2 cups bottled garlic chilli sauce
1 white onion, chopped
2 green chillies, sliced
Vinegar and sugar to taste

Heat 1 tbs oil in a medium-sized pot. Brown garlic and pork. Add dark soya sauce and sugar and allow to caramelise. Add light soya sauce and water and bring to the boil. Add hard-boiled eggs. Turn down fire to simmer pork till tender, about 20 minutes. Remove meat and eggs to cool.

In the meantime, prepare the other ingredients. Heat another 4 tbs oil in a wok and brown the soya bean cakes and the flour rolls. Drain on kitchen towels and set aside.

Bring another pot of water to boil and cook squid. Drain. Remove hard beak and spine. Dice cucumber, fish cakes, spiced flour rolls, squid, belly pork and egg. Combine all the diced ingredients in a bowl.

Cut the soya bean cakes in half and cut a pocket along the cut side. Fill pocket with diced mixture. Garnish with coriander leaves and serve with the chilli dip, drizzled with the braising sauce.

GU BAK KWAY TEOW [For 10-12]

This Singapore (actually Teochew) dish has a stock fragrant with galangal and full of beefy goodness. And no wonder, for you can find tripe, tendons, brisket and shin in the soup. This was the version sold by the popular stall at Hock Lam Street since the 20s.

400 g (approx 12 oz) brisket or shin beef
300 g (approx 9 oz) beef tendon
300 g (approx 9 oz) cleaned beef tripe, scalded
400 g (approx 12 oz) oxtail, cut into pieces
4 thick slices lengkwas (galangal)
1 tbs grated gula malacca (palm sugar) or soft brown sugar
1 tsp dark soya sauce
$1^1/_2$ tbs salt or to taste
A handful of pepper corns
300 g (approx 9 oz) beef fillet, sliced
800 g (approx 1.5 lb) kway teow (flat rice noodles)
500 g (1 lb) bean sprouts

Garnish:
1 head kiam chye (large stemmed salted mustard
     greens), cut into strips
1 bunch Chinese celery, chopped

Chilli dip:
Chilli sauce (bottled sambal olek is convenient)
Lime juice, salt and sugar to taste
A knob of young lengkwas (galangal), pounded till fine

In a pot large enough to accommodate the meats, bring 3-4 litres of water to the boil. Place tendons, tripe (scalded first) and oxtail into the pot, together with the lengkwas, gula malacca, soya sauce and salt.

Simmer for two to three hours or till meat is tender, skimming off fat and scum from time to time. Add brisket or shin halfway through and continue to simmer till tender. Remove meats from the pot. Taste stock and adjust seasoning. When meats are cool, cut into bite-sized pieces.

Bring another pot of water to the boil. Scald loosened noodles and bean sprouts. Drain. To serve, place noodles, bean sprouts and a selection of cooked meats in a bowl. Top with slices of raw beef fillet and pour over boiling stock. Do this twice over if you prefer your meat well cooked.

Garnish with kiam chye and Chinese celery and offer a chilli dip topped with pounded lengkwas on the side.

Of course the name associated with Hainanese chicken rice was Swee Kee, that famed two-storeyed coffee shop along Middle Road where the chicken came with great ginger and chilli sauces, enriched with gasp, chicken fat! The shop is no more, and gone too is its airy tiled dining room, cooled by ceiling fans and an interior airwell, where you eat at marble-topped tables and sit on bentwood chairs.

HAINANESE CHICKEN RICE

[For 8-10]

1 chicken, approximately $1^1/_2$ kg (3 lb)
2 cucumbers, peeled and sliced
2 stalks coriander leaves, chopped roughly
1 tsp salt
2 stalks of spring onions, knotted
1 thumb-length knob of ginger, bruised
5 whole garlic cloves, bruised with skin

Rice:
4 cups rice
4 cups chicken stock
3 whole garlic cloves, with skin
2 slices ginger
2 tbs oil or chicken fat
1 tsp salt
4 pandan leaves, knotted

Sauce:
10-12 red chillies
2 cloves garlic, peeled
Lime juice
Salt and sugar to taste
$^1/_2$ cup chicken stock or cooked chicken fat
3 thumb-length knobs of ginger
Salt and sugar to taste

Rub 1 tsp salt all over chicken and stuff cavity with spring onions, ginger and garlic. Bring water in a pot large enough to submerge the chicken to boil. Place chicken into the pot and allow water to come to the boil again. Reduce heat, cover and simmer for another half an hour.

Remove chicken and plunge into a basin of cold water to obtain silky skin. Rub oil all over chicken and set aside. Set aside stock to flavour rice and chilli and ginger sauces.

Process ginger and $^1/_4$ cup of stock or fat in a blender till fine. Season with salt and sugar to taste. Now process chillies with remaining stock and garlic. Add salt, sugar and lime juice to taste. Set aside.

To cook the rice, heat oil or chicken fat in a wok and brown garlic and ginger. Add washed rice grains and fry till fragrant. Add stock and cook in a rice cooker together with pandan leaves till dry and fluffy.

Chop chicken into pieces and garnish with coriander. Serve with rice.

LOH KAI YIK

[For 10]

If you are old enough, this hawker who sold this pink Cantonese stew of braised chicken wings in fermented soya bean sauce would be part of your food memories. He was so fat, he sold his food sitting on a tricycle with a large pot before him. From this pot, he would fish out your choice of meat and snip it with a pair of scissors. A trusty assistant pedalled him around everywhere but it was his nasal cry that we still remember.

4 tbs vegetable oil
4 cloves garlic, chopped
4 shallots, sliced
8 cubes of nam yee (soya cheese)
4 tbs taucheong (brown soya bean paste)
1 kg (2 lb) belly pork
15 chicken wings
300 g (approx 9 oz) pig's intestines,
    rub thoroughly with salt, washed
$^1/_2$ cup red or brown hoisin sauce
2 tbs sugar
100 g (approx 3 oz) pig's skin, bristles removed
150 g (approx 5 oz) pig's liver
4 processed ju her (cuttlefish)
20 tau pok (tofu puffs)
400 g (12 oz) kangkong (water convolvulus), blanched,
    knotted into small bundles
$^1/_2$ tsp salt

Sauce:
Bottled chilli garlic sauce or mix pounded fresh chilli with
    bottled sweet chilli sauce, light soya sauce and lime juice.

Heat oil in a pot large enough for the stew. Saute till fragrant but not browned, the garlic, shallots, nam yee and tau cheong. Brown the pork, chicken wings and intestines in this mixture. Add water to cover, flavour with hoisin sauce and bring to the boil.

Skim surface of soup scum, turn down fire to simmer and add the whole piece of pig's skin, liver, cuttlefish and soya bean puffs. Leave to cook till tender and remove ingredients from the pot. Taste stew to adjust seasoning. Add the kangkong to warm and remove.

To serve, slice meats and cut cuttlefish and soya puffs into bite-sizes pieces. Place on a bed of kangkong and ladle over the gravy. Serve with white rice and chilli sauce on the side.

HAE MEE [For 8]

500 g (1 lb) medium-sized prawns
500 g (1 lb) pork ribs, chopped into large pieces
1 pig's tail, chopped into large pieces
10 cups of water
300 g (approx 3 oz) lean pork in one piece
1 tbs salt
1 tbs brown sugar
1 tbs light soya sauce
1 tsp belacan (shrimp paste)
1 tsp chilli powder
500 g (1 lb) fresh Hokkien yellow noodles
300 g (approx 3 oz) dried rice vermicelli (beehoon),
    soaked to soften
300 g (approx 3 oz) bean sprouts
300 g (approx 3 oz) kangkong (water convolvulus)

Garnish:
Fried sliced shallots
5 red chillies, sliced
Crisp pork lardons (fried cubes of lard), optional

The story goes that cabaret girls and their clients would frequent the famed prawn noodle stalls along Hokkien Street. They did a roaring late-night business in the 1940s through to the 1960s. And since there were competing stalls, there would be endless arguments on which sold the best one. Aside from the noodle soup, you could also order the soup with just pig's tail or bean sprouts and kangkong (water convolvulus). And these were no bland treats, for you would be offered chilli powder and cut chillies to add to your bowl.

Stock: Detach heads of prawns. Reserve. Place pork ribs, pig's tail and 10 cups of water in a large pot and bring to the boil. Boil prawns briefly. Remove, using a strainer and peel. Reserve prawns and shells.

Heat 2 tbs oil in a wok and stir-fry prawn heads and shells till fragrant. Add belacan and chilli powder and continue to fry over a low fire till aroma is released. Add two ladles of stock into the wok and simmer for half an hour. Switch off fire and strain shrimp stock back into the pot. Season with salt, sugar and soya sauce.

Boil piece of lean pork in the same pot. Remove when cooked – pierce with a fork to check if juices run clear. When cool, slice and reserve. Taste stock and adjust seasoning. Poke pork ribs and tail with a fork. If tender, switch off fire.

Noodles: Boil another pot of water. Scald noodles and softened vermicelli for a minute or two. Drain. In the same pot, scald bean sprouts and kangkong for half a minute. Drain.

To serve: Place two kinds of noodles in a bowl with some bean sprouts and kangkong. Top with prawns, pork slices and pork ribs or tail. Pour over hot soup and garnish with fried shallots and crisp lardons. Eat with a dip of sliced red chilli and light soya sauce and more chilli powder dusted on top.

OR LUAK [For 4-6]

There are wet and dry versions of this oyster omelette, often prepared by hawkers with generous addition of tapioca and rice starch. This version uses just a litle starch and can be browned according to taste.

6 eggs
2 tsp fish sauce
1 tbs chopped garlic
2 tbs tapioca flour, 1 tbs. rice flour and a pinch salt,
    rendered in $^1/_2$ cup of water
1 cup small oysters or 4-6 large fresh oysters
1 tsp chilli, powder, flakes or paste
Fresh coriander sprigs
Bottled chilli sauce, mixed with vinegar to taste

Beat eggs in a bowl till fluffy. Add fish sauce to season. Leave aside.

Heat frying pan till hot. Add 1 tsp oil. Pour in half of the thin batter and allow it to set.

Pour egg mixture over the flour pancake. Leave to set for about 10 seconds, then add more batter followed by 1 tbs of oil to allow parts of the omelette to brown. Cook a further 2-3 minutes. Cut into quarters and turn over to brown the other side. Remove.

Add 1 more tbs of oil. Saute chopped garlic and chilli till fragrant, but not browned. Toss in the oysters, add a pinch of salt and stir quickly. Serve atop omelet garnished with coriander leaves and a dip of vinegared chilli sauce.

JU HER ENG CHYE [For 5]

This water convolvulus salad with cuttlefish and jelly fish is an early childhood memory, dating back to when I was four. Sold by an itinerant hawker, I used to wait for him to pass where we lived at Mohamed Sultan Road. It was one of those foods sold at stalls whenever there was a wayang playing. But you could also buy a great version at Chinatown, where a diminutive ma chieh would peddle plates of a brilliantly green vegetable and succulent cuttlefish, redolent with sesame oil, at the five-foot way.

250 g (8 oz) kangkong (water convolvulous)
$^1/_2$ cured ju her (cuttlefish)
4 tau pok (tofu puffs)
100 g (apporx 3 oz) seasoned jellyfish
Roasted white sesame seeds

Sauce:
1 tbs seasoned vinegar
1 tbs chilli powder.
$^1/_2$ cup hoisin sauce
A few drops of good quality sesame oil
2 tbs onion oil

First make the onion oil. Zap 1 tbs ready fried shallots (available bottled) in half cup of oil in the microwave oven on high for a minute, then leave for a while for the shallot flavour to infuse the oil.

Cut off roots of kangkong and wash thoroughly to remove grit. Pluck off leaves and snap stems into short lengths. Bring a pot of water to the boil and scald trimmed kangkong.

Plunge vegetable into cold water to stop the cooking process. Drain well. Cut cured cuttlefish into strips - scald briefly in boiling water. Drain. Slice tau pok into strips.

To serve, place a mound of boiled kangkong on a plate. Top with cuttlefish strips, jellyfish and tau pok. Scatter sesame seeds over the lot. Dress with chilli, hoisin sauces and fragrant oils.

FRIED HOKKIEN MEE [For 8-10]

It may be called Hokkien Mee, but you will not find it in Fujian. Its old-time name was Rochore Mee, because it was created in the 1930s by a Hokkien ex-seaman who had his stall on Rochore Road. This is a late-night dish, sold by stalls that operate only after dinner time.

200 g (7 oz) medium prawns
300 g (approx 9 oz) belly pork
2 squids
4 fishcakes, sliced
1-2 tbs chopped garlic
500 g (1 lb) fresh flat yellow Hokkien noodles
300 g (approx 9 oz) bean sprouts
1 tsp fish sauce
1 small bunch Chinese chives, cut into short lengths

Parboil pork in a pot filled with six cups of water. Remove pork, cool and cut into strips. Reserve. Peel prawns. Boil prawn shells in the pork stock. Keep raw prawns for use later.

Clean squid by removing head and ink sacs. Remove skin, then boil whole squid in pork stock. When squid turns colour, remove and cut into rings. Reserve.

Heat 2-3 tbs oil in a wok large enough for the noodles. Sauté garlic till fragrant but not browned. Add pork strips, then peeled prawns. When prawns turn pink, add prepared stock. Season with fish sauce and a shake of white pepper.

When stock comes to the boil, add bean sprouts. Bring to the boil again and add noodles, fish cake and squid. Toss well to combine. Add fresh chives, warm through and serve with sliced red chilli or chilli paste and some lime halves.

Hints: Fresh Hokkien noodles are already salted, so be restrained with the seasoning.

YU TOW MAI FUN [For 8-10]

This Fish-head Beehoon Soup has a characteristic milky look, because it is laced, with just that — milk! It has been a late-night supper dish since the 1950s.

500 gm (1 lb) dried thick beehoon (rice vermicelli)
1 threadfin fish head, about 1.5 kg (3 lb),
    chopped into pieces
2-3 tbs oil or lard
2 cloves garlic, chopped
8-10 slices ginger
8 cups of fresh or canned unsalted chicken stock
1 tbs Chinese rice wine
1 tbs light soya sauce
1 tbs salt
1 tsp sugar
300 g (approx 9 oz) chye sim (Chinese flowering cabbage)
1 tsp sesame oil
2 cups low fat milk or soya milk

Marinade:
$^1/_2$ tsp salt
Pepper to taste
1 tsp rice wine

Garnishes:
Fried pork lardons
Coriander leaves
Pickled green chilli

Bring a kettle to the boil and soak dried beehoon in boiling water till it softens. Drain. Place noodles in bowls. Rub salt into chopped fish head to get rid of the fishiness. Wash off salt and marinate fish with rice wine for about 15 minutes.

Heat 2 tbs oil in a pot. Brown fish head pieces. Remove fish from pan, drain and fry garlic and ginger, adding more oil if needed, till fragrant, but not browned. Add stock. Season with rice wine, soya sauce, pepper, salt and sugar. Bring soup to the boil. Scald green vegetables in the soup and remove.

Add the milk and stir until it comes to the boil to prevent curdling. Return fish to the pot. Finish with a drizzle of sesame oil. Taste and adjust seasoning.

Top noodles with fish pieces and green vegetables, pour over hot soup and serve garnished with crisp pork lardons, fresh coriander leaves, and pickled green chilli on the side.

CHAR KWAY TEOW
[For 6-8]

Teochew fried noodles is laden with salt, lard and all things bad, but it is a beguiling dish for which Singaporeans living abroad come back to get a fix.

$^1/_2$ cup vegetable oil or lard
1 tbs chopped garlic
2 Chinese sausages, sliced
1 fish cake, sliced
100 g (3 oz) medium prawns, peeled
300 g (approx 9 oz) fresh kway teow (flat rice noodles)
1 tsp salt
2 tbs dark soya sauce
1 tbs light soya sauce
4 eggs, beaten
300 g (approx 9 oz) bean sprouts
1 tbs chilli paste or use bottled sambal chilli
1-2 tbs sweet dark soya sauce
100 g (3 oz) shelled cockles, optional
1 small bunch of chives, cut into short lengths

Do not wet noodles before use or the dish will be soggy. Heat large wok till smoking hot. Add half the oil and fry garlic till fragrant. Add the sausage, fishcake and prawns. Fry for a minute. Move ingredients to the side of the wok and add loosened noodles. Season with salt, and soya sauces. Mix well.

Move noodles to the side of the wok and add 1 tbs of oil in centre of wok. When hot, fry the chilli paste. Pour in the beaten eggs, and scramble them. Add the bean sprouts, the chives and the cockles, if using. Toss to combine. Serve hot.

INDIAN ROJAK

[For 6-8]

Indian rojak is nothing like rojak as most of us know it. It is a mixture of deep fried battered items tossed together with shredded cucumber, bangkwang (yam bean) and green chilli in a cooked sweet potato sauce. Not found in India, it is unique to this region and has a special place in the hearts of those who have eaten it at the long gone Indian food stalls at Waterloo Street, so popular in the 1960s.

BASIC BATTER

    1 kg (2 lb) plain flour, sifted
    1 tbs salt
    1 tsp baking powder
    2 tbs sugar
    1 tsp pepper
    4 cups water

Make up a batter with the ingredients above, taking care to add the water slowly into the mix. Leave to rest for one hour. This basic batter is used to make the various items that make up the rojak.

PLAIN FRITTERS

    1 cup of basic batter
    1 large onion, finely chopped
    2 green chillies, finely chopped
    Enough oil for deep-frying

Add onion and chilli to the batter. Heat oil in wok and spoon out balls to deep-fry until golden brown. Drain on kitchen paper and cut into quarters.

COCONUT FRITTERS

    1 cup basic batter
    2 tbs rice flour
    $^1/_2$ cup grated coconut
    1 tbs dried prawn, chopped
    Flour
    Oil for deep-frying

Add rice flour and grated coconut to the basic batter. Set aside for 10 minutes to form a soft dough. Using floured hands, shape dough into 8-10 cm long rolls. Heat oil and deep fry fritters till golden brown. Drain on kitchen towels.

PRAWN FRITTERS

    2 cups basic batter
    300 g small prawns
    A few drops of red food colouring
    Oil for deep-frying

Combine prawns, food colouring and batter. Take spoonfuls of the battered prawns and fry in heated oil till golden. Drain on kitchen paper.

TAPIOCA FRITTERS

    2 cups grated tapioca
    Fried shallots
    A pinch of turmeric powder
    A pinch of salt
    Oil for deep-frying

Mix grated tapioca with the other ingredients above. Form into rolls. Heat oil in wok and fry rolls till brown. Drain on kitchen paper.

continued overleaf ...

GRAVY

3 tbs vegetable oil
10 dried chillies, softened first in hot water
1 cup shallots
1 tsp belacan (shrimp paste)
2 medium-sized sweet potatoes, boiled then mashed
2 cups water
2 tbs tamarind paste made with 1 cup water
Sugar to taste
1 tbs salt
1 tbs toasted sesame seeds

Process chillies, shallots and shrimp paste till fine. Heat 3 tbs oil in a pot and fry spice paste over medium fire till fragrant. Add mashed sweet potato, together with small amounts of the water, to aid in the blending.

Add tamarind water, salt and sugar. Bring to the boil, stirring to ensure sauce does not burn. It should be of a thick consistency. Top with sesame seeds just before serving.

OTHER SALAD INGREDIENTS

2 pieces taukwa (firm soya bean cake), fried
2 hardboiled eggs, cut into wedges
1 whole cured cuttlefish
2 boiled potatoes, peeled
1 tsp chilli powder
A pinch of salt
1 tbs oil
1 bunch Chinese lettuce leaves
1 bangkwang (yam bean)
1 cucumber
2-3 green chillies
2 purple onions

Heat oil in a wok and fry whole cuttlefish till cooked. Toss with chilli powder and a pinch of salt. Remove and cool. Toss boiled potatoes in the same pan to absorb the rest of the chilli dressing. Remove. Shred lettuce leaves, yam bean and cucumber. Slice green chilli and onions.

To serve: Cut the various fritters into small pieces. Do the same with the taukwa, eggs, cuttlefish and potatoes. Top with the shredded vegetables and serve with hot gravy on the side.

NGO HIANG [Makes about 15 rolls]

Another wayang food stall that has become a food centre staple. Around the centrepiece of a Hokkien spiced pork roll, grew a selection of fried items ranging from kwan chiang (a shocking pink pork sausage), taukwa (firm soya bean cake), prawn fritters, fish balls to even black century eggs, It was a colourful spread indeed, especially with its red chilli and pink flour sauce dips. Fried vegetarian bee-hoon used to complete the dish.

1 tbs oil
5 shallots, sliced
500 g (1 lb) pork mince
300 g (approx 9 oz) medium prawns, peeled, de-veined and chopped coarsely
10 water chestnuts, peeled and chopped
1 egg

1 tsp five-spice powder
1 tsp salt
1 tsp sugar
1 tsp black soya sauce
Pepper to taste
1 tbs corn flour

1 large dried bean sheet, cut into 15 equal rectangles
1 tbs corn flour made into a thin paste with a little water
Oil for deep-frying

Heat 1 tbs oil in wok and fry shallots till golden. Set aside. Mix pork, prawns, water chestnuts and egg in a basin. Season with salt, sugar, black soya sauce and five-spice powder. Blend in corn flour and finally, add the fried shallots and shallot oil. Mix well to combine.

Wipe both sides of bean sheets with a damp cloth to rid it of excess salt. Place a small mound of meat mixture in the middle of the sheet. Roll up like a spring roll. Use corn flour paste to seal. Place rolls on a heatproof plate and steam for 10 minutes or so in covered wok. Cool.

Heat oil in a wok. Deep fry rolls till brown and crisp. Slice and serve with chilli sauce.

NASI LEMAK [For 6]

The cry of nasi lemak echoing up and down the HDB corridors must be a part of most people's childhood. But long before the days of public housing, Malay boys, carrying oversized baskets, were already hawking this breakfast food at Malay enclaves round the island. Now the boys have given way to Chinese stallholders who offer a plethora of fried items to go with the simple coconut rice.

COCONUT RICE

3 cups uncooked rice
2 cups of water
$^1/_2$ tsp salt
1 pandan leaf, knotted
1 cup coconut cream

Wash and drain 3 cups of rice. Cook rice with water, salt and a knotted pandan leaf in a rice cooker, together, till liquid is absorbed. Now stir in the cup of coconut cream, cover and allow the rice to absorb its fragrance. Use a fork to fluff up rice grains before serving.

SAMBAL IKAN BILIS

$^1/_4$ cup vegetable oil
2 cups dried ikan bilis (anchovies)
2 purple onions, peeled
1 clove garlic, peeled
8 dried red chillies, soaked first to soften
1 tsp belacan (shrimp paste)
1 tbs sugar
1 tsp tamarind paste, mixed with 4 tbs water

Heat oil in a wok and fry the dried anchovies over medium heat until they are crisp. Remove fish from the pan and drain on kitchen towels.

Process softened chillies, garlic, onion and belacan to make a paste. Wipe wok clean using a kitchen towel. Heat another 1 tbs oil in wok. Fry chilli paste till brown and fragrant. Add sugar and tamarind water. Fry for another minute or two.

Return ikan bilis to the wok, when ready to serve, mixing everything well together.

To assemble, ladle some rice on the plate, serve with sambal ikan bilis, simple fried fish or omelette and sliced fresh cucumber.

LONTONG [For 10]

Lontong is actually pressed rice cakes, which the Malays cook in large cylinders. But to most Singaporeans, lontong is rather the dish of rice cakes and vegetables in a coconut gravy that is eaten for breakfast. A Malay dish now enjoyed by all races, it can easily be found in food courts, unlike the past when it was sold only in the morning markets.

1 cup shallots, peeled
1 tbs belacan (shrimp paste)
1 tsp turmeric powder
4 tbs dried prawns
2 buah keras (candlenuts)
5 dried chillies or 1 tsp chilli powder
600 ml (2.5 cups) coconut milk,
    add water to make 2 litres (8 cups)
6 tau kwa (firm soya bean cakes), cut into half and fried
$^1/_2$ medium-sized cabbage, shredded
300 g green beans, sliced
2 carrots, shredded
1 yam bean, peeled and shredded
10 hardboiled eggs, peeled
1 tbs salt
2 tbs sugar
1 cylinder of pressed rice cake,
    cut into wedges

Process finely shallots, shrimp paste, dried prawn, buah keras and dried chillies (the last two ingredients soaked first in hot water to soften) using a food chopper or mortar and pestle. Mix in the turmeric powder.

Heat 2 tbs vegetable oil in a pot large enough to accommodate the vegetables and brown the spice paste over a moderate fire till fragrant. Add the shredded vegetables, the fried soya bean cakes and enough water to barely cover the vegetables. Add salt and sugar.

When it starts to simmer, add the coconut milk, stirring all the time till it comes to the boil to prevent the milk from curdling. Add the eggs and simmer for another 15 minutes. Taste and adjust seasoning if needed.

To serve, place rice cakes (warmed first by steaming), soya bean cakes and an egg on a deep plate. Pour over the gravy and some vegetables and serve, sprinkled with a spicy coconut dressing called serondeng (see recipe on this page) and with bottled sambal chilli on the side.

SERONDENG [Makes 1 cup]

1 cup grated coconut, without skin
1 tbs bottled sambal chilli
4 kaffir lime leaves
A pinch of salt
1 tsp sugar

Discard the tough spine of the kaffir lime leaves and using a pair of scissors, finely shred the leaves.

Mix bottled sambal and kaffir lime threads into the grated coconut and mix evenly. Stir in salt and sugar.

Spread coconut mixture on baking tray and roast in an oven at 100˚C until it is golden and toasty. This roasted coconut can be kept indefinitely in the fridge.

KETUPAT

Ketupat, traditionally served with satay and nonya or Malay curried dishes

Ketupat are pressed rice cakes which are traditionally cooked and served in its own coconut leaf or pandan leaf packet. Here I improvise with a small cloth bag, about the size of a sock, which could be sewn up from white cotton, or cut up from an old-fashioned cloth coffee strainer, failing which new cotton socks would do as well.

If you need a large quantity of ketupat, fill several of these cloth bags, instead of filling one large bag which would make cooking and handling difficult.

Fill bags with uncooked white rice up till three-quarters full, tie up the opening with a length of kitchen twine. Put the bag in a pot and make sure that the rice is evenly distributed throughout the length of the bag. Add water and a knotted pandan leaf into the pot to lend its fragrance to the rice and boil for 2 hours.

Leave to cool, untie the string and simply roll down the fabric to remove the rice cake. Cut the ketupat into squares or rounds depending on the recipe.

Lim Kee's goreng pisang could be Singapore's unofficial consumer price index. Costing seventy cents each two decades ago, a large goreng pisang in 2013 costs $1.20.

NASI BRIYANI [For 8]

Islamic and Jubilee restaurants are names from the past. At these two-storeyed coffee shops, both along North Bridge Road, we learnt how to eat classic Indian Muslim dishes such as briyani — saffron rice cooked with either curried chicken or mutton.

Chicken:
4 tbs ghee or oil
1 cup shallots, sliced
1 large onion, chopped
1 thumb-sized length of ginger, chopped
4 cloves garlic, chopped
1 tsp chilli powder
1 tsp turmeric powder
1 tsp cumin powder
2 tomatoes, chopped
2 tbs chopped mint leaves
1 tbs salt
$1^1/_2$ kg (3 lb) chicken pieces
2-3 cardamoms
5 cm cinnamon
4 tbs yoghurt

Rice:
4 cups Basmati rice
1 tbs oil or ghee
4 cloves garlic, smashed
1 thumb-sized length ginger, smashed
5 shallots, finely chopped
5 cm stick cinnamon
5 cardamoms
5 cloves
1 tsp saffron threads
Sprinkling of rose essence
1 tsp salt
4 cups fresh or canned unsalted chicken stock

Chicken: Heat oil in a wok and fry the shallots till golden. Set aside. In the same oil, brown the chopped onion, garlic and ginger. Add a little water to the spice powders to make a paste and add it to the wok to fry over a low fire till fragrant.

Add the tomatoes, mint and salt and cook till softened. Finally add the chicken pieces, cinnamon and cardamoms. Cook gently till meat is just cooked. Stir in the yoghurt and cook for 15 minutes more. Reserve chicken and gravy and skim oil to flavour the rice.

Rice: Wash and drain the rice. Heat oil in a wok. Fry ginger, garlic and shallots till light brown. Add the cinnamon, cloves and cardamoms. When fragrance rises, add the reserved oil and rice grains. Continue to fry till grains absorb the oil.

Heat stock and add salt, saffron and rose essence. Pour stock over the rice. Transfer rice to a rice cooker and cook till just dry.

Make a well in the centre of the rice for the chicken. Cover with rice and cook, without stirring, for another 10 to 15 minutes. Garnish with the fried shallots and serve.

GORENG PISANG [For 10]

Again a Koek Road speciality that has been going strong for more than 50 years. Lim Kee's goreng pisang, now operating at Maxwell Market, are still sweeter and crisper than most, both desired qualities of this local fried banana fritter that is said to have originated from the Malay fried banana dessert, jemput jemput.

10 ripe bananas (pisang rajah is best)
100 g (approx 3 oz) plain flour
50g (approx 1.5 oz) rice flour
1 tsp baking powder
Pinch of salt
1 tsp vegetable oil
About 1 cup water
Oil for deep-frying

Sift flours, baking powder and salt into a basin. Make a well in the middle of the flour and add the oil and a little water.

Work in flour from the sides to make a smooth mix, then add the rest of the water or enough to make a batter that will coat the back of a wooden spoon.

Heat a wok half full with oil. Peel bananas and dip into batter. When oil is smoking hot, deep fry battered bananas two or three at a time till golden brown. Use a slotted spoon to lift fritters and drain on kitchen paper. Best eaten hot.

GREEN BEAN OR
RED BEAN SOUP

[For 6-8]

This is the version sold by hawkers. Variations include adding sago and coconut milk to the green bean soup and lotus seeds and dried orange peel to the red bean soup.

250 g ($^1/_2$ lb) red or green beans
8 cups water
250 g ($^1/_2$ lb) rock sugar
4 pandan leaves, knotted

Soak red or green beans for half an hour. Drain. Place soaked beans into a large pot together with the water and boil till tender and swollen. Add sugar and pandan leaves and simmer, stirring often till it comes to a boil. Serve hot or at room temperature.

SWEET POTATOES IN
GINGER SYRUP

[For 6-8]

This was a favourite if simple dessert found at foodstalls that used to accompany the travelling Chinese wayang (opera). Such a typical Chinese dessert stall would offer this and other dessert porridges made from beans and preserved and dried fruit (recipes follow). Again a vanishing treat.

500 g (1 lb) sweet potatoes
1 knob of ginger, smashed
1 cup sugar
4 cups water

Place sugar in a pan and add water and crushed ginger. Bring to the boil and leave aside for ginger to infuse the syrup.
   Steam sweet potatoes in a container set above a saucepan of water. When soft, remove and cool. Peel and cut into chunky pieces and soak in ginger syrup for at least an hour before serving. Serve hot or cold and thin down syrup, according to taste.

CHENG TNG [For10]

Originally a cleansing health soup, over the years it has developed into a full-blown dessert, complete with shaved ice and coloured jelly. The old-time version, originally sold at wayang stalls, should have the five essential ingredients of barley, longans, dried persimmons, gingko nuts and lotus seeds in it.

   100 g (approx 3 oz) China barley
    20 gingko nuts, peeled and cored, from supermarkets
$^1/_2$ cup lotus seeds
100 g (approx 3 oz) dried longans
1 tai hau lam fruit, from Chinese medical halls
6 dried persimmons, sliced
50 g (approx 2 oz) dried agar agar strips,
     soaked in cold water
4 pandan leaves, knotted
200 g (7 oz) rock sugar
8 cups water

Soak the tai hau lam fruit till it expands. Remove peel, veins and grit. Soak agar strips in cold water.

   Bring water and sugar to boil in a large pot. Add the ingredients in this order, barley, gingko nuts, lotus seeds, and cook till tender. Add pandan leaves, dried longans, expanded fruit and persimmon strips and simmer for 15 minutes. Finally, add the agar agar strips and serve at once.

COOPERATED ASSOCIATION

SINGAPORE FUSION

Mixing and matching

WHOEVER WOULD HAVE THOUGHT that Chinese noodles, western potatoes, bottled tomato sauce and Indian spices put together could result in mee goreng, an enduring Singapore favourite? It is just one of the many Singapore dishes that have borrowed ingredients and ideas from everywhere to become food classics.

Long before fusion food became fashionable, Singapore cooks were already mixing and matching in the kitchen — the Malays borrowed from the Chinese, the Indians from the Chinese and the Chinese from both these groups. And everybody owed something to the Portuguese, who introduced important spices, chilli and tamarind, from faraway South America and Africa, as well as passed on their predilection for marinating foods with lime, lemon and vinegar.

The Portuguese, in fact, played a major role in influencing the cuisines of not only Singapore but the region, judging from the similar dishes based on common spices such as tamarind, coriander and chilli found in their colonies or ports of call at Goa, Malacca, Ambon and Macau.

As Armando "Pinky" Sa Silva, a Macanese wrote "a lively trade already existed between Amoy and Malacca at the time the Portuguese arrived there in 1509. Hokkien merchants, seamen and craftsmen took native wives. In time, a distinctive Malaccan-Hokkien cuisine developed. It was the forerunner of today's Nonya Cuisine".

> *The entire branch of gutsy nonya food is a successful marriage of mostly Chinese and Malay cooking styles.*

As with the Hokkiens, Portuguese and Goanese men took native wives. In the seventeenth century, Christian Malaccan women and their off spring provided the basic ethnic stock of many old-line Eurasian families. Such cross-cultural influences make it fascinating to trace the roots of any Singapore dish.

Chilli crab, for instance, is a Singapore hybrid for you can find Chinese bean paste, Malay chilli and western tomato sauce in the recipe. And nowadays, the preferred crab is Sri Lankan and not the domestic mud crabs! The same sort of mix can be seen in fishhead curry, murtabak (both not found in India) and indeed all the dishes in this chapter, which are but a sampling of the fabulous results that occur when cross influences are given free reign.

Indeed the entire branch of gutsy nonya food is a successful marriage of mostly Chinese and Malay cooking styles, while another robust match among the Portuguese, Indians, Malay and Chinese in turn resulted in Eurasian cuisine. The Portuguese contributions aside, the Chinese, must we thank for adding foodstuffs such as noodles and soya bean products to our kitchens. The fresh spice pastes that have become so much a part of our cooking we owe to the Malays while the Indians taught us how to cook with aromatic spices such as turmeric, cardamoms, cumin and cloves. Together, they make up quite an array of ingredients to experiment with, and so our foremothers did, with quite delicious results.

While we take these dishes for granted — they are our everyday foods, after all — they should also be valued and preserved, for few, if any, food cultures can boast of such extensive and varied roots. Ours is a truly unique culinary heritage.

ROJAK [For 10]

Whoever would have thought that Chinese hawkers could so successfully take a salad originating from Indonesia and give it an inimitable twist. Called *rudjak* in Indonesian, our rojak has yu tiao (Chinese dough sticks), cured cuttlefish, tau pok (soya bean puffs) and even century egg in it. The simpler Javanese version consists mainly of fruits and vegetables.

1 small cucumber, cut into wedges
2 slices pineapple, cut into wedges
$^1/_2$ small bangkwang (yam bean),
   peeled and cut into wedges
1 cup bean sprouts, blanched
A bunch kangkong (water convolvulus), blanched
2 century eggs, peeled and quartered
Half a cured ju her (cuttlefish), cut into pieces
1-2 fried yu tiao (Chinese dough sticks)
2-3 tau pok (soya bean puffs)

Dressing:
2 heaped tbs hayko (black prawn paste)
Hot water to soften
2-3 red chillies, pounded
  (or use 1 tbs bottled sambal olek)
1-2 tbs sugar or to taste
Tamarind water (1 tsp tamarind paste and $^1/_4$ cup water)
Juice from 1 lime
$^1/_2$ cup roasted peanuts, chopped finely
Tip of a bunga siantan (pink ginger bud), grated finely

In a bowl, soften the black prawn paste first with a few spoonfuls of hot water. Add chilli, tamarind water, sugar and lime juice to the softened prawn paste, stirring all the while to blend into a thick sauce. Finally, add the chopped nuts and bunga siantan. Taste to adjust seasoning. There should be a balance of salty, sour and sweet.

Cut the cucumber, pineapple and bangkwang into bite-sized wedges. Blanch the bean sprouts and kangkong in a pot of boiling water or microwave them on high for two minutes. Place yu tiao and tau pok in an oven on low 100°C heat for 10 minutes to make them crispy. Cut into small pieces.

Assemble the salad by placing the vegetables into a bowl, followed by the century egg and cuttlefish. Top with crisp yu tiao and tau pok. Dress with peanut and prawn paste sauce, mix well and serve at once.

TAUHU GORENG [For 8]

Soya bean cake is a Chinese product but see how the Indonesians and the Malays have made it over into gutsy tauhu goreng. Originally street food, this substantial salad uses tau kwa (firm soya bean cakes) and not tofu (soft soya bean cakes) despite its name.

> 5-6 tau kwa (firm soya bean cakes)
> Oil for deep-frying
> 1 cucumber, shredded
> 3 cups bean sprouts, scalded
>
> Peanut sauce:
> 2 cloves garlic
> 2-3 chilli padi (bird's eye chilli)
> 1 cup roasted peanuts, chopped
> $^1/_2$ cup tamarind water
>   (mix 1 tbs tamarind paste into $^1/_2$ cup of water)
> 2 tbs sugar
> 1 tbs dark soya sauce
> $^1/_2$ tsp salt

Fry tau kwa in hot oil till lightly browned. Drain on kitchen paper. In the meantime, pound garlic and chilli till fine. Place chilli mixture in a mixing bowl and add peanuts, tamarind water, salt, sugar and soya sauce. Blend well, adding more water if needed.

Cut taukwa into squares. Top with cucumber and bean sprouts. Pour over peanut sauce just before serving.

ROTI JOHN [For 2]

The question is who was the John for whom this dish was named? Was John just an ordinary Englishman who asked for a sort of French toast at a Malay stall and the hawker obliged? Whatever the answer, this version of fried bread with the robust addition of onions, chilli and minced meat is now a part of our heritage.

> 1 small French loaf
> 2 eggs
> $^1/_2$ large onion
> 100 g (approx 3 oz) minced beef or chicken
> 4 green chillis
> Salt and pepper to taste
> Oil for frying

Chop onion and green chillis. Break eggs into a bowl and beat. Stir in the chopped chillis, onion, minced meat and salt and pepper to taste.

Cut French loaf into thick slices. Coat bread slices on one side with egg mixture.

Heat 2 tbs oil in flat fry pan. When hot, place bread, meat side down, into the oil. Press down bread for egg mixture to adhere. Leave for a few minutes, then turn over to brown the other side.

Remove from pan and drain on kitchen paper. Fry the other slices of bread in the same manner, adding more oil if necessary. Serve hot with fresh cut cucumber and bottled sweet chilli sauce.

SARDINE SAMBAL [For 4]

A Malay innovation and truly Singaporean. Who else would match tinned sardines with a sambal? Best, it has become a favourite offering at Malay rice stalls.

> 1 tin sardines (425 g, 14 oz) with tomato sauce
> 1 tbs oil
> 1 onion, sliced
> 4 red chillies, pounded OR 1 tbs chilli powder
> 2 tomatoes, chopped
> 1 stalk lemon grass, white stem portion, bruised
> $1/_2$ tsp salt
> 1 tsp sugar
> Juice from 2 limes

Heat oil in a wok. Fry onions, tomato, chilli and lemon grass till onions are translucent. Add the entire contents of the tin. Season with salt and sugar. Squeeze lime juice over, remove lemon grass and serve with rice.

AYAM TEMPRA [For 6-8]

This recipe is for chicken cooked in soya sauce and lime juice. However, you can use the same recipe for fish or pork.

> 500 g (1 lb) chicken, cut into pieces
> 1 large onion, sliced
> 1 tbs dark soya sauce
> $1/_2$ tsp salt
> 1 tbs sugar
> $1/_2$ cup water
> 2 red chillis, sliced
> 2 green chillis, sliced
> Juice from two limes

Heat 2 tbs oil in a wok and fry onions till soft and browned. Brown the chicken pieces. Season with dark soya sauce, salt and sugar. Allow to caramelize, then add water to the meat.

When chicken is tender, add the sliced red and green chillis and add lime juice just before serving. If liked, garnish with some shredded lime peel for extra fragrance.

PORK VINDALOO
[For 8-10]

The use of vinegar in this and the next Eurasian recipe can be attributed to the Portuguese, though the Indonesians too have semur dishes where a spiced soya sauce, with tamarind, is the main flavouring. The roots of this dish can be traced to Goa, where vindaloo, a vinegared curry, had its origins and was probably brought to Malacca in the sixteenth century.

1 kg (2 lb) marbled pork, cut into pieces
2 tbs oil, butter or ghee
1 tsp mustard seeds
1 large onion, chopped

Blend together:
8 dried chilies, softened first in hot water
5 cloves garlic
1 thumb-sized piece of ginger

1 cup vinegar
1 tbs cumin powder
$^1/_2$ tsp nutmeg powder
1 tbs mustard powder

1 cinnamon stick
4 cloves
4 cardamoms
1 tbs salt or to taste

Blend softened chillies, garlic and ginger in a blender together with the vinegar. Add powdered spices to the mixture in a bowl. Rub spice paste into pork pieces.

Heat oil in an acid-resistant pot like enamel or Corning ware. Fry mustard seeds till they pop. Add onion and fry till soft and fragrant.

Add pork pieces, together with the blended spice paste, the whole spices and brown. Moisten with a cup of water. Season with salt. Turn down heat and simmer till pork is cooked. Taste to adjust seasoning, adding 1 tbs sugar if desired.

A fusion food that has reached Singapore through long distances in place and time: The vinegar that characterises this dish was the wine vinegar that Portuguese sailors used to pickle pork for their voyages.

SEMUR [For 8-10]

Look at what the Eurasians have done to beef stew! Just like the Indonesian version, it comes spiced and vinegared and is best eaten with lots of rice and sambal belacan.

I kg (2 lb) stewing beef, cut into large pieces
2 tbs vegetable oil
2 large onions, quartered
2 cloves garlic, crushed
3 tbs thick black soya sauce
1 tsp salt
1 tsp black pepper
1 tbs sugar
1 tbs vinegar
1 stick of cinnamon, about 6 cm
4 star anises
10 cloves
4 cardamoms
4 potatoes, peeled and cut into large pieces
4 carrots, peeled and cut into large pieces
2 tomatoes, quartered

Heat oil in a pot large enough for all the ingredients. Brown onions and garlic, then the beef. Season with thick black soya sauce, salt, pepper, sugar and vinegar. Add the whole spices. Toss to brown the beef surfaces.

Add enough water to just cover the meat. Bring to the boil, then reduce heat. After an hour, add the root vegetables. Simmer till meat is tender.

Add tomatoes and cook till softened. If gravy seems too thin, make a paste from 1 tbs corn flour mixed with a little water and stir it into the stew till it thickens.

DEVIL CURRY [For 8-10]

A Eurasian chicken stew that evolved from the Portuguese. You can find western ingredients such as sausage, roast pork or beef, even a ham bone in it and plenty of Asian spice – chillies, ginger and mustard seeds to add fire to the pot, as befits its name. A festive dish, it is cooked usually at Christmas time and is eaten with white rice.

$1^1/_2$ kg (3 lb) chicken, cut into pieces
2-3 tbs oil
1 thumb-sized piece of ginger, julienned
1 tsp black mustard seeds
4-6 large onions, chopped
4 cloves garlic, chopped
5 tbs chilli paste or 10 dried chillies,
     softened in hot water, then pounded
4 tomatoes, roughly chopped
$^1/_2$ tsp belacan (shrimp paste)
$^1/_2$ tsp kunyit (turmeric) powder, optional
1 tsp lengkwas (galangal) powder, optional
4 potatoes, peeled and quartered
5 pork sausages, cut into two
1 cucumber, cored and cut into large pieces
3 green chillies, left whole
100 g (approx 3 oz) Chinese roast pork, optional,
     cut into thick slices
1 tbs salt
1 tsp sugar
Juice from 1 lemon

Heat oil in a pot large enough for the stew ingredients. Fry ginger strips till browned. Remove. Now fry the mustard seeds until they pop. Add the onion and garlic, followed by the chilli paste and tomatoes, then the belacan and powdered spices.

When spices are fragrant, brown the chicken pieces. Add water to just cover the meat — the chicken and vegetables will give off their own juices — season with salt and sugar and bring to the boil. Cook for 10 minutes.

Add potatoes and sausage and turn down fire to simmer till chicken is tender. Finally add cucumber, green chillies and roast pork, if using. Leave for a while for flavours to mature and squeeze in lemon juice just before serving.

BABI ASSAM GARAM [For 8-10]

The Portuguese also influenced nonya food as seen in this tamarind pork. While the main influence in Chinese nonya food is Malay, here Portuguese Goa, with its strong notes of tamarind, vinegar and coriander, dominates. The cooking style of boiling, then frying meat is also typically Portuguese. Incidentally, you will find the same flavours in Macau cooking, for they share a common Portuguese heritage.

I kg (2 lb) belly pork
2 tbs tamarind paste
1 cup of water
1 tbs salt
$^1/_2$ tsps sugar
Oil for frying

Using tweezers, pluck clean the pork skin of bristles. Make up a tamarind marinade by mixing the tamarind paste with water. Add salt and sugar to make a thickish consistency. Marinate the pork in this mixture overnight covered in the fridge.

The next day, boil pork in marinade over a moderate fire till meat is tender.

Just before serving, cut the pork into fairly thick slices. Heat 1 tablespoon of oil in a fry pan and brown the pork slices in batches to ensure even browning. Cook down marinade in the pan to make a thick marmalade. Serve with a dip of chopped garlic and vinegar.

SEK BAK [For 8-10]

500 g (1 lb) belly pork or stewing pork
10 tau pok (soya bean puffs)
4 hardboiled eggs
2-3 tbs oil
4 cloves garlic, smashed
2 lengkwas (galangal) slices
2 tbs dark soya sauce
1 tbs light soya sauce
1 tsp salt
1 tbs sugar
1 cinnamon stick (about 10 cm)
5 cloves
2 star anise

Salad ingredients:
2 cucumbers, sliced diagonally
Fresh coriander leaves
Green chillies, sliced
1 onion, chopped

Chilli sauce:
6 red chillis, pounded
2 cloves garlic, pounded
2 tbs bottled chilli sauce
Juice from 4 limes
Sugar and salt to taste

Heat oil in a large pot and brown garlic cloves and galangal slices. Add whole piece of pork and season with soya sauces and sugar. Fry till sugar caramelizes.

Toss in aromatic whole spices and salt and pour enough water to just cover the pork. Bring to the boil. Turn down fire and simmer till tender. Stew hardboiled eggs and soya puffs in the sauce for 15 minutes more till gravy is thickened.

When cool, slice pork, cut soya puffs into four, and quarter the eggs. Make up chilli sauce by mixing together ingredients. Taste and adjust seasoning, if needed.

To serve, place stewed meats and salad ingredients in a bowl and top with chilli sauce. Toss and garnish with coriander sprigs. Eat on its own or as part of a meal.

While the Chinese cook a similar braised pork stew, it is the Eurasians who have turned up the heat in their way of preparing this dish. It appears with plenty of fresh green chillis, red chilli sauce and crunchy cucumbers in the mix!

PORK SATAY [For 8-10]

The Chinese-Malay mix is closely intertwined here, even if pork is found in this nonya satay. The usual peanut sauce is also given a lift by fresh pineapple puree.

500 g (1 lb) lean pork
200 g (7 oz) pork fat
1 stalk lemon grass, slice the white stem portion only
1 tsp coriander powder
4 buah keras (candlenuts), soaked in water to soften
8 shallots, peeled
2 red chillies
$1/_2$ tsp belacan
1 tsp salt
1 tbs sugar
1 cup coconut milk
1 tbs oil
Bamboo skewers, soaked first in water to prevent burning

Peanut sauce:
1 cup roasted peanuts
1 stalk lemon grass, slice white stem portion only
2 red chillis
8 shallots, peeled
$1/_2$ tsp belacan (shrimp paste)
4 buah keras (candlenuts), soaked in water to soften
2 tsp tamarind paste, mixed with $1/_2$ cup water, strained
1 tbs oil
1 tsp salt
1 tbs sugar
Optional: 2-3 finely shredded kaffir lime leaves
1 small can crushed pineapple

Blend lemon grass, buah keras, shallots, chillis and belacan with the coconut milk. Add coriander powder, salt and sugar.

Slice the pork and pork fat into small pieces and marinate in spice paste for at least one hour.

To make the sauce, blend lemon grass, chilli, shallots, buah keras and belacan together with tamarind water. Chop roasted nuts. Heat oil in a small pot and fry spice paste until fragrant. Add salt and sugar, then the nuts and kaffir lime shreds. Leave aside. Blend pineapple to a pulp.

Thread marinated pork and fat onto soaked skewers. Baste with oil and grill over glowing charcoals until seared in parts. Serve satay with sliced onions, cucumber, ketupat (see page xx) and peanut sauce, topped with chopped pineapple.

CHAP CHYE [For 10]

It is remarkable how the nonyas could take an essentially Chinese cabbage stew and make it gutsy and full-bodied. One can just picture the Malay wife of an early Chinese immigrant trying to replicate this dish in her own fashion! The peranakan taste for robust flavours must come from this early Malay influence and it shines through here despite the Chinese ingredients used throughout.

1 Chinese cabbage, cut into fairly large wedges
2 tbs oil
4 rounded tbs tau cheow (brown soya bean paste)
1 tbs chopped garlic
200 g (7 oz) belly pork
200 g (7 oz) medium prawns, peeled and de-veined
10 dried Chinese mushrooms
$^1/_4$ cup mok yee (dried black jelly fungus)
$^1/_4$ cup dried lily buds
10 sheets tim chok (dried sweet bean curd sheets)
5 fu chok (dried soya bean sticks)
2 bundles dried glass noodles
1 tbs dark soya sauce
1 tsp salt
Pepper to taste

Soak mushrooms and reserve the soaking water. Soak the other dried foods in a fresh bowl of water. When softened, drain and keep aside. Snip off the mushroom stems and the hard ends of the lily buds and the black fungus. Cut soya bean sticks and sheets into bite-size pieces.

Bring a small pot of water to boil and parboil pork in it. Remove pork and reserve stock. When cool, slice pork and leave aside.

Heat oil in a large pot. Brown garlic and soya bean paste. Add pork slices and peeled prawns, then the mushrooms, fungus, bean curd sheets and sticks.

Add the cabbage, then the stock and mushroom water. If needed, top up with more water. The liquid should just cover the ingredients. Bring to the boil and add the rest of the ingredients. Season with salt and pepper.

When cabbage and dried foods are soft, finish off with a swirl of soya sauce to deepen the colour. Serve hot with rice and sambal belacan on the side.

Macau also has a dish called Lacassa, made with shrimp and thick rice noodles, but without coconut milk, as does Penang where it comes in a tamarind gravy. Then there is Singapore's, but whichever the dish, all are fusion noodles.

In the Singapore version, for example, the rice noodles are Chinese, the fresh spice paste, Malay and the fresh herb, *daun kesom*, originally Vietnamese.

Another clue – laksa stems from a Sanskrit word *laksha* for "hundred thousand", referring perhaps to the long list of ingredients called for in the dish.

Instead of making spice paste from scratch, substitute with bottled sambal chilli and add coriander and turmeric spice powders to the paste.

LAKSA [For 10]

500 g (1 lb) medium prawns
2 cups shallots, peeled
20 dried chillis, softened in hot water
1 tbs belacan (shrimp paste)
3 tbs dried shrimp, soaked for a while in water to soften
10 buah keras (candlenuts)
1 tsp turmeric powder
1 tbs roasted coriander powder
2 stalks lemon grass, white stem portion, crushed
4 tbs oil
4 cups coconut milk
2 tbs salt
1 tbs sugar
Pepper
500 g (1 lb) dried thick rice noodles
300 g (approx 9 oz) bean sprouts, scalded
200 g (7 oz) dried glass noodles, scalded and drained

Garnishes:
4 fresh red chillis, pounded
Salt to taste
1 cucumber, peeled, cored and shredded
4 fried fishcakes, sliced
1 bunch daun kesom (laksa leaves), finely shredded
100 g (approx 3 oz) see hum (fresh cockles), optional

Boil a pot of water and cook prawns till they turn pink. Remove, shell prawns when cool and reserve prawns and stock. Process shallots, chillis, belacan, dried shrimp and buah keras in a chopper till fine. Add powdered spices to the paste.

Heat oil in a pot large enough for the gravy. Brown spice paste and add lemon grass stalks, adding a little water from time to time to prevent burning, until oil rises to the surface. Add prawn stock, followed by coconut milk, stirring all the time to prevent curdling till it comes to the boil. Season with salt, sugar and pepper to taste.

Boil some water in another pot and boil dried noodles till *al dente*. Drain and divide noodles among bowls. Top with a little softened glass noodles and bean sprouts.

Garnish with a prawn, fishcake slices, shredded cucumber and daun kesom. Pour over hot coconut gravy and serve with a dollop of pounded chilli mixed with a pinch of salt.

FISH HEAD CURRY [For 6-8]

An Indian innovation, created for the Chinese — for who but a Chinese, would eat curried fish heads? It is textural eating, itself a Chinese eating trait, and indeed, you cannot find this curry in India.

It is attributed to Gomez of Gomez fish head curry fame. Today, the torch has been passed on to Muthu's at Race Course Road, who buys kurau (threadfin) fish heads, instead of just using throwaway heads, to cook this Singapore classic.

1 large fish head, about $1^1/_2$ kg (3 lb)
4 tbs oil
2 large onions, chopped
4 cloves of garlic, chopped
1 thumb-sized length of ginger, chopped
1 cup fish curry powder, made into a paste with water
2 cups coconut milk, thinned down with 2 cups water
4 tbs tamarind paste mixed with 2 cups of water, strained
1 tbs salt
1 tbs sugar
2 sprigs curry leaves
10 ladies fingers
4 tomatoes, cut into quarters
4-5 red and green chillies

Rub fish head with salt, then wash it thoroughly to rid it of fishiness.

Heat oil in a large wok and soften onions, garlic and ginger. Add curry paste and brown over a low fire till oil rises to the surface. Sprinkle a little water if the paste is in danger of burning.

Add the coconut milk, a little at a time, then the tamarind water, salt, sugar and curry leaves. Bring to the boil, stirring all the time. Add whole fish head to the wok, together with chillies, tomatoes and ladies fingers.

Simmer for another 15 minutes or till fish is cooked. Serve hot with boiled rice.

MEE REBUS
[For 8-10]

Another Malay dish employing Chinese yellow noodles, it also has Chinese soya bean cakes in a spicy sweet potato gravy.

500 g (1 lb) fresh Hokkien yellow noodles
500 g (1 lb) bean sprouts
200 g (7 oz) shin beef
200 g (7 oz) prawns

Spice paste:
10 dried chillies, softened in hot water
1 cup shallots, peeled
1 tsp belacan (shrimp paste)
10 slices lengkwas (galangal)
1 tsp turmeric powder

Gravy:
200 g (7 oz) sweet potato, boiled, peeled and mashed
1 heaped tbs tau cheow (brown soya bean paste)
1 tbs salt
2 tbs sugar

Garnishes:
5 hardboiled eggs, sliced
4 tau kwa (firm soya bean cake), diced and fried
Fried shallots
10 limes, halved
4 green chilli, sliced
Dark soya sauce, optional
Toasted grago (shrimp fry), optional

Make a stock by boiling beef in 6 cups of water till tender. Remove and slice beef. Cook prawns in the stock. Peel prawns and set aside. Reserve stock.

Process spice paste ingredients in a chopper till fine. Heat 2 tbs oil in a wok and fry spice paste till oil rises to the surface. Add tau cheow and fry till fragrant. Add the stock, mashed sweet potato, salt and sugar and cook over a low fire till all is amalgamated. Taste to adjust seasoning if needed.

Cook one serving of noodles and bean sprouts in a wire ladle in boiling water. Remove, drain and place on a plate. Top with beef slices and prawns.

Pour hot gravy over and garnish with egg wedges, soya bean cake, shallots, chilli and a halved lime. Drizzle some dark soya sauce if desired and sprinkle some grago, browned earlier in a slow oven till crisp.

MEE SIAM [For 10]

There is a plethora of Malay dishes that uses Chinese noodles, fried with spice pastes, creating totally different taste sensations from the original.

The Thai connection for Mee Siam is uncertain, despite the name, though the gravy is tart and sweet as in many Thai dishes. There are versions of this originally Malay dish which relies on Chinese noodles and soya bean cake. The nonya version below is possibly the most popular.

500 g (1 lb) dried beehoon (rice vermicelli),
    soaked in cold water till softened, drained
500 g (1 lb) bean sprouts
300 g (approx 9 oz) prawns, shelled and deveined
5 tau kwa (firm soya bean cakes), diced
Oil for deep-frying
2 cups water

Sambal (spice paste):
2 cups of peeled shallots
60 dried chillies, deseeded, soaked in hot water to soften
3 tbs belacan (shrimp paste)
4 tbs dried shrimp
2 tbs sugar
1 tsp salt or to taste

Gravy:
1 large onion, sliced into rings
6 tbs tau cheow (brown soya bean paste)
3 tbs heaped tamarind paste,
    mixed with a cup of water, then strained
7 cups water
5 tbs sugar
1 tbs salt or to taste
1 cup stock, made with the prawn shells

Garnishes:
10 eggs, hardboiled
A handful of chives, cut into short lengths
10 limes

Peel prawns and set aside. Boil shells in 1 cup water until shells turn pink. Strain and reserve stock.

Heat a wok quarter full with oil and fry diced tau kwa in batches till they brown. It will take some time, but this can be done a day before. Leave aside. In a chopper, process shallots, softened chillies, belacan, dried shrimp till fine.

Heat half cup of oil left over from the frying of the tau kwa. Brown spice paste till oil rises to the surface. Add sugar and salt. Divide this paste into three lots.

To make gravy, place one lot of spice paste into a large pot. Add the tau cheow, tamarind juice, prawn stock, sugar and salt. Pour in the water and bring to the boil. Adjust seasoning to taste. It should be sweet and sour. Set aside.

Fry the second lot of spice paste in a wok, add the prawns, followed by the bean sprouts. Pour in 2 cups of water and bring to the boil. Push ingredients to one side and place beehoon into the gravy. Cover with ingredients and allow beehoon to cook for a few minutes, then mix well.

To serve, pour hot gravy over beehoon and garnish with wedges of hardboiled egg, chives and browned tau kwa cubes. Offer a halved lime and some of the last lot of sambal on the side.

Note: To make it less spicy, de-seed soaked chillies first, using gloves. Instead of making the spice paste from scratch, Glory nonya sambal belacan makes a good substitute. Just add dried shrimp.

INDIAN MEE GORENG [For 8-10]

This is the innovative dry Indian Muslim version of fried noodles where Chinese wheat noodles are fried with Indian spices and yes, western ingredients of tomato sauce and potatoes.

> 500 g (1 lb) fresh Hokkien yellow noodles
> 2 –3 tbs oil
> 2 large onions, sliced
> 1 tbs chilli paste OR chilli powder
> 1 tsp curry powder
> 2 potatoes, skinned and sliced thickly
> 1 bunch Chinese flowering cabbage (chye sim),
>   cut into small pieces
> 2 tomatoes, quartered
> 300 g (approx 9 oz) bean sprouts
> A pinch of salt
> 1 tsp dark soya sauce or to taste
> 1 tbs bottled tomato sauce
>
> Garnish:
> Red and green chillies, sliced
> Fried shallots

Heat oil in wok. When hot, saute onions till soft. Add chilli paste and curry powder. Keep stirring over a low fire to ensure no sticking. Sprinkle a little water to prevent burning.

Turn up fire to medium. Add vegetables — potato first, followed by the greens, tomato and bean sprouts. Season with a pinch of salt.

Loosen noodles and add to the wok. Add soya sauce and tomato sauce. Mix thoroughly. Sprinkle a little water, if needed, for easier mixing. Garnish with fresh chillies and fried shallots. Serve immediately.

PONGGOL MEE GORENG [For 8-10]

Even more innovative than Indian Mee Goreng. Chinese stallholders took the dish over and now we have Chinese mee goreng that comes wet with a spicy seafood sauce.

500 g (1 lb) fresh Hokkien yellow noodles
1 large onion
2 cloves garlic
1 tbs chilli paste or chilli powder
1 tsp belacan (shrimp paste)
2 tbs dried shrimp
2 tbs bottled tomato sauce
100 g (3 oz) medium-sized prawns, peeled and deveined
100 g (3 oz) squid, cleaned and cut into rings
3 eggs
1 tsp salt
1 tsp light soya sauce
1 cup of seafood stock or water
5 stalks chye sim (Chinese flowering cabbage),
   cut into short lengths

Process onions, garlic, chilli, belacan and dried shrimp in a food chopper.

Heat oil in a hot wok. Turn down the fire and brown spice paste. When fragrant, turn up the fire and toss in the prawns and squid. Season with tomato sauce, salt and soya sauce. Add stock or water and bring to the boil.

Toss loosened noodles into the sauce. Make a space in the middle. Break eggs into this space and scramble. Add greens, mix well and serve at once.

CHILLI CRAB [For 6-8]

Punggol seafood. The name brings to mind chilli crab, crispy baby squid and seafood mee goreng. All three dishes were probably created by Choon Seng Restaurant, which started life in a coffee shop right at the end of Ponggol Road. The place is no more, but the dishes have remained popular for over three decades. Today, every seafood restaurant offers this troika of Singapore classics, which has Chinese, Malay and even Indian influences.

3 live mud crabs, about 500g (1 lb) each
4 tbs vegetable oil
2 purple onions
2 cloves garlic, chopped
1 thumb-length of ginger
2-3 red chillies
2 ripe tomatoes, chopped
1 heaped tbs tau cheow (brown soya bean paste)
1 tbs sugar
Light soya sauce, if desired

Put crabs to sleep by placing them for an hour or so in the freezer. Bring a pot of water, large enough to submerge the crabs to boil. When water comes to a rolling boil, cook crabs for about five minutes or till they turn pink. Remove with tongs and plunge into cold water to stop the cooking process.

Cut away the strings that tie up the claws, pull off the shell by prying under the underbelly flap. Remove the head sac, found within the shell, and the spongy gills. Using a knife, detach the claws and cut the body into four, or more parts, if the crab is large. Use a pestle to crack the claws. Leave aside.

Now make the sauce. Put onions, ginger, garlic and chilli in a food processor and chop till fine. Heat oil in a wok. When hot, saute the mixture till fragrant, then add the tomatoes.

Leave to cook till caramelised, then add tau cheow and sugar. Stir well and allow to simmer, adding a little water if it seems too thick, till the flavours amalgamate.

Now add the crab and toss to coat the pieces with the sauce. Taste, and season with a drizzle of light soya sauce, if needed. Top with chopped Chinese celery and serve immediately with crusty bread on the side.

SPICED MUTTON CHOPS [For 6]

These are no ordinary mutton chops. Long gone, they live in the memory of those who frequented Ujagar Singh's. This was a second-floor eatery in St Gregory's Lane off Coleman Street, famed for its deep-fried mutton chops that came deliciously spiced. The recipe is an approximation of the remembered taste, which was not entirely Indian nor Western, despite the use of chops.

> 6 mutton chops
> 5 tomatoes, chopped
> 2 slices of ginger, finely chopped
> 2 cloves garlic, finely chopped
> 2 green chillies
> $1/_2$ cup coriander leaves, chopped
> $1^1/_2$ cups yoghurt
> 1 tsp garam masala
> 1 tsp chilli powder
> 1 tbs coriander powder
> Pinch of nutmeg
> 1 tsp salt
> 3 tbs ghee or oil

Cover chops with tomatoes, ginger, garlic, chilli and coriander leaves in a pot. Add a little water to prevent sticking and cook, covered, simmering till the liquid dries up.

Mix the dry spices of garam masala, chili powder, coriander powder and nutmeg into yoghurt. Add salt. Coat the chops with this mixture and leave at least 30 minutes to allow the spices to penetrate the meat.

Heat oil or ghee in a pan and fry chops on both sides till brown. Serve with mint chutney on the side and garnished with coriander leaves and lemon halves.

Ujagar Singh in his old-world restaurant and kitchen. The famous eatery, known even to the US Marines, closed in the early 1990s.

A pattie of belacan from Malacca and a block of Penang belacan.

BARBECUED FISH IN BANANA LEAF [For 6-8]

You see these barbecued seafood stalls at every hawker centre. The stallholders are Chinese but the recipe is Malay, even if the spice paste is a mish-mash! The accompanying dip is also a new-fangled way of eating the salted shrimp fry called chinchalok.

Chincalok or salted shrimp fry is a Malay condiment, the making of which has spread to the Peranakan Chinese. A mixture of salted tiny shrimp or *grago*, which also forms the basis for belacan, is allowed to ferment in bottles until a pink sauce redolent of the scent of anchovies, results. Usually eaten with fried fish, the Chinese stallholder instead serves it with beef noodles and yes, barbecued fish. In these cases, the salted shrimp is mixed with a dollop of chilli sauce, rather than fresh cut chillies, fresh onions and lime juice.

    500 g (1 lb) sting ray
    1 tsp salt
    1 onion
    1 tsp belacan (shrimp paste)
    2 chillies
    2 cloves garlic
    1 stalk lemon grass, white stem portion
    $^1/_2$ tsp sugar
    1 large banana leaf

Put onions, chilli, belacan, garlic and lemon grass in a chopper and process roughly. Scald banana leaf with hot water to make it pliable.

Rub salt all over fish, and place it on a softened banana leaf. Spread spice paste over the top of the fish. Wrap leaf over fish and secure with toothpicks or metal staples.

Either grill under a hot fire or barbecue fish over coals for 10 minutes on each side.

CRISPY BABY SQUID [For 10]

You either love or hate this sweet, well-seasoned crunchy dish which, together with chilli crab, is a Singapore creation.

500 g (1 lb) baby squid, the smallest you can find
1 cup bottled sweet chilli sauce
1 tbs dark soya sauce
1 tbs sugar
1 tsp salt
Oil for deep-frying

Heat a wok half filled with oil till smoking hot. Dry squid with paper towels and deep fry till lightly golden. Remove and drain on paper towels. Remove oil, leaving 1-2 tbs in the wok. Heat wok again and this time, fry squid in the mixture of sweet chilli sauce, dark soya sauce, salt and sugar until they caramelize and turn crispy. Serve at once.

MISO CLAMS [For 6-8]

Actually a time-honoured chi-char dish, Akashi Restaurant at Tanglin Shopping Centre has fused Singapore and Japanese styles to create a bestseller.

2 kg (4 lb) white clams
3 tbs chopped garlic
2 tbs brown miso
1 tsp sugar
2 red chillis, sliced
$^1/_2$ cup mirin (Japanese sweet rice wine)

Swish clams around in several changes of water, scrubbing it well to rid it of grit. Soak for about half an hour to allow grit to float. Drain well.

Heat 2 tbs oil in a wok. Brown garlic and miso till golden. Add sugar. Remove browned mixture, including oil. Set aside.

Heat wok up again. When smoking, add clams and pour over mirin. Cover and cook for about five minutes. Lift cover and remove opened clams on a plate. Leave unopened clams to cook for another minute or so. Discard if shells are still tightly shut after this.

Pile clams onto plate and top them with the mixture of miso and garlic. Garnish with sliced red chillis.

A new era in Singapore eating

ETHNIC SUPERMARKET

THE AGE OF THE WORKING WOMAN. Asian convenience foods, machine helps and prepared foods come into their own. A new era has begun for Singapore eating. Food has to be prepared without too much trouble. Who has the time to buy and then to haul out mortar and pestle to pound the long list of fresh spices called for in recipes such as otak-otak? Who can be bothered to go on to make the popia skin after the laborious effort of shredding and cooking the vegetables for the filling? The supermarkets and food retailers respond to this need.

In the early 1970s, shelves began to be stocked with Asian bottled helps that go beyond the chilli, tomato and soya sauces of previous years. This gathered momentum over the years with prepared foods such as wonton and spring roll wrappers and even green chendol strips appearing to provide even more short-cuts in food preparation. It never used to be so. You could not buy even a red chilli in the supermarket before. And if you needed coconut milk, you had to buy fresh grated coconut to squeeze for its milk.

Now Asian vegetables such as bitter gourd are stocked in the vegetable section of the supermarkets, various kinds of soya bean cakes and fishballs can be found in the cold section and there is even a special area devoted to Asian dried products and sauces. As for that coconut milk, it now comes powdered in packets or liquid in tetrapaks and cans. And in the freezer section, you can find packets of roti prata, prawn dumplings and glutinous rice balls nestling next to the frozen peas, waffles and potato cakes.

The focus turns to making a dish taste as fresh as possible in spite of the commercial preparations relied upon in making it.

With bottled helps and half the food preparation done for the cook, recipes have changed accordingly. The list of ingredients called for is short. Few recipes now require you to make the wonton wrapper before giving instructions on how to make the filling or ask you to scrape the meat from the fish in order to obtain fish balls. Instead, the focus turns to making a dish taste as fresh and authentic as possible in spite of the commercial preparations relied upon in making it. The best cook becomes the one who can turn out such well-loved foods with little effort and yet can disguise the commercial flavours. Or the one who can make inventive use of these new convenience helps and yet hold fast to favourite tastes.

Just by looking at the array of products on the shelves, it becomes clear what are the most popular dishes in Singapore. Laksa and mee siam pastes proliferate as do bottled sambal chilli, the most versatile of Asian bottled pastes. To use it in a variety of dishes, simply add powdered spices according to the recipes. And there does not seem to be an end to the trend with new convenience foods appearing on the shelves, the latest being chicken rice seasoning in a bottle!

In tandem with this trend comes an interest in foreign foods. With better education and greater earning power, Singaporeans have become well-traveled people. With their regular trips to Southeast Asian countries, America, Japan, Europe and Australia, comes an appreciation of foods from the world over. And again this is reflected on the shelves as food retailers scramble to meet this most recent consumer demand. Thus, not only convenience, but also that much-touted attribute, globalization, has hit the Singapore table.

ROASTED SPARE RIBS [For 10]

These roasted ribs are marinated with bottled hoi sin sauce which is a sweetened paste made from soya beans. It replicates the sweet rich flavours of the Cantonese roast meats, another traditional favourite, without too much trouble.

> 250 g (8 oz) bottle of hoisin sauce
> 2 cups dried soya beans, soaked in water for at least 1 hour
> 2 kg (4 lb) spare ribs, chopped into large pieces
> 1 tbs sesame oil
> 2 tbs rice wine
> Black pepper

Place ribs in a baking tray and pour over the hoisin sauce. Drizzle over sesame oil and rice wine. Grind some black pepper over. Leave covered at least four hours if not overnight in the fridge. This is not essential but it does tenderize the meat greatly.

Boil the soaked beans in a pot of water till they are tender. Mix them with the marinated ribs.

Heat oven to 200°C. Place tray of ribs and beans, covered with foil, in the middle of the oven. Roast for 15 minutes, then turn down heat to 180°C and cook for another hour or so. Remove foil during the last 15 minutes to brown top.

OTAK-OTAK [For 8-10]

No pounding of spices, no squeezing of milk from coconut, no scraping of fish to get fish meat. Today, you can get the sambal (spice paste) from a bottle, the coconut milk from a packet and the fish meat in tubs from the markets, to make this savoury fish custard of Malay origin.

> 2 cups of minced fish meat
> 1 packet of coconut cream (200 ml, 7 fl oz)
> 1 tbs bottled sambal chilli paste
> 1 tbs coriander powder
> 1 tsp turmeric powder
> 4 large eggs
> 1 tsp sugar
> White pepper to taste
> 2-3 kaffir lime leaves, shredded (optional)
> Banana leaf, scalded to soften, or 2 turmeric leaves,
>   to line the baking pan

Place fish meat into a large basin. Add coconut cream, then the bottled sambal, turmeric and coriander powders. Break eggs into the basin as well. Add the sugar; no need for salt as the fish meat is generally salted already. Using a handheld blender or a whisk, mix everything together till it becomes a smooth paste.

Line a square shallow baking tray with a banana or turmeric leaf. Pour spicy custard over. Using scissors, snip fine threads of the kaffir lime leaves over the top.

Place baking pan in an oven tray, filled with water, and bake in a moderate oven 180°C till top is golden and custard is set. It should take about 30 minutes. Pierce with a skewer to test. If it comes out clean, the otak is done.

Remove pan from the oven in order not to dry out the custard and cover with a piece of foil if you're not serving it immediately.

SAYUR LODEH

[For 6-8]

Singaporeans have taken the originally Indonesian dish of sayur lodeh to heart and it now frequently appears at hotel and catered buffets. Who can resist vegetables cooked in a spicy coconut gravy? Made here with bottles spice paste, fresh herbs such as kaffir lime leaves hide any processed flavours.

1 large purple onion, chopped
2 cloves garlic, chopped
2 tbs bottled sambal chilli paste
1 heaped tsp turmeric powder
$1/2$ cup dried prawns
2 stalks of lemon grass, white stem portion, bruised
4 tbs oil
1 small bangkwang (yam bean), thickly shredded
1 small carrot, thickly shredded
1 cup French beans, cut into short lengths
$1/4$ cabbage, cut into bite-size pieces
1 brinjal, cut into large pieces
4 tau kwa (firm soya bean cakes), quartered
2 cups water
2 cups coconut milk
1 tbs salt
1 tbs sugar
Kaffir lime leaves

Heat oil in a large pot and soften onion and garlic. Add the bottled sambal paste, then the dried shrimp. When fragrant, add the turmeric powder and the lemon grass.

Brown the vegetables that need more cooking first: the bangkwang, followed by the carrots and the brinjal. Pour in enough water to just cover the vegetables and allow to come to the boil.

Reduce heat, add the softer vegetables: cabbage, beans and the tau kwa. Finally add the rest of the water and thicken with coconut milk, stirring all the time to prevent curdling till gravy comes to the boil again. Season with salt and sugar and serve with hot rice.

You can serve extra bottled sambal on the side for those who like the dish hotter.

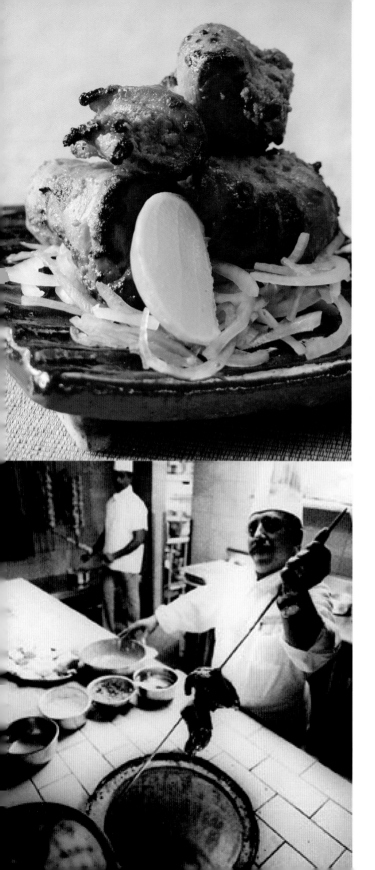

TANDOORI CHICKEN [For 6-8]

While south Indian tastes prevail on this island, the Omar Khayyam restaurant (now closed) at Hill Street introduced us to northern Indian food. It was a culture shock - the place was plush and posh unlike the rough and ready charm of its banana leaf cousins. As for its signature dish, chicken tandoori (chicken roasted in a clay tandoor or oven) we took to it with gusto. It is still a popular dish when eating North Indian nosh some 30 years on, hence the selling point of bottled tandoori paste.

> l kg (2 lb) of chicken pieces, skin removed
> 3 heaped tbs tandoori paste (Patak's is good)
> 200 g tub of plain yoghurt
> 1-2 tsp chopped garlic
> 1-2 tsp chopped ginger
> 1 stalk fresh coriander leaves
> 1 lemon, cut into wedges

Marinate skinless chicken in yoghurt mixed with the tandoori paste (which comes already salted), ginger and garlic for at least four hours if not overnight, covered in the fridge.

Place marinated chicken pieces on an oven tray and roast in a 200°C oven for 20-30 minutes or till burnt in parts. Serve hot, garnished with fresh coriander leaves and wedges of lemons on the side.

Note: This goes well also with raita, a yoghurt based dip made from mixing plain yoghurt with shredded cucumber, a pinch of salt and pepper.

FRENCH BEANS WITH BLACK OLIVE PASTE

[For 8-10]

500 g (1 lb) French beans
200 g (7 oz) minced pork
1 tbs oil, taken from bottle of olive paste
4 cloves garlic, chopped
2 tbs bottled black olive paste
$^1/_2$ tsp sugar
Salt and pepper to taste

Top and tail beans and cut each bean into two or three. Heat oil taken from the bottle in a wok and when hot, brown garlic and minced pork. Add beans, cook for a few minutes over high heat. Turn down the heat and add the olive paste. Season with salt, sugar and pepper and serve immediately.

It was Her Sea Thai restaurant (now closed) along Orchard Road that introduced Thai Olive Rice to Singapore back in the 1980s. It was a hit. And to think that the olive paste is actually a traditional Teochew condiment, eaten with rice porridge or used as a flavouring, such as in flash-fried French beans.

THAI OLIVE RICE

[For 8-10]

5 cups of uncooked white long grain rice
5 cups water
500 g (1 lb) minced chicken or pork
4 cloves of garlic, chopped
1 bottle (250 g, 8 oz) of black olive paste
1-2 tsps fish sauce
Generous shake of white pepper

Garnishes:
1 cup of pine nuts or peanuts, roasted
5-6 fresh basil leaves
2 fresh red chillies, sliced
1 thin-skinned lemon, diced finely

Wash the rice and cook with the water in a rice cooker till dry and fluffy. While rice is cooking, prepare the garnishes.

Take two tablespoons of oil from the bottle of olive paste and heat in a wok. Saute chopped garlic till fragrant, then add the olive paste. Add the meat, fish sauce and lots of white pepper. Cook over high heat, tossing well.

Dish out cooked rice onto a platter. Top with olive/meat mixture and garnish with nuts, chillies, lemon bits and basil leaves. Before serving, toss rice, dressing and garnishes well together.

CHICKEN GREEN CURRY [For 8-10]

With Bangkok being a favourite weekend retreat for Singaporeans, bottled green curry paste - made from lemon grass, green chilli, galangal and coriander - soon found its way to shop shelves in Singapore. Be warned, it is fiery hot, so a little goes a long way! As with the use of all bottled pastes, adding fresh herbs goes a long way in freshening up the flavours.

$1^1/_2$ kg (3 lb) chicken, chopped into large pieces
1 onion, chopped
1-2 tbs green curry paste
2 tbs oil
2 cups coconut milk
$^1/_2$ cup water
4 fresh kaffir lime leaves
2 stalks lemon grass, white stem portion, bruised
2 fresh red chillies, sliced into two or three
2 fresh green chillies, sliced into two or three
10-12 fresh basil leaves
1 tbs fish sauce
2 brinjals, cut into pieces
    or a cup of Thai pea aubergines

Heat oil in a large pot. Fry onions till translucent. Add the curry paste and fry till aroma arises. Add the chicken to brown, then throw in a couple of kaffir lime leaves and lemon grass stalks to scent the pot.

Add $^1/_2$ cup of water and bring to the boil. Add the brinjals, reduce heat and simmer till they soften. Finally, add the coconut milk, stirring all the time till it boils to prevent curdling.

Season with fish sauce and garnish with chillies, kaffir lime and basil leaves before serving.

GREEN CURRY PIZZA [For 8-10]

1 large frozen pizza crust
2 tbs green curry paste
2 tomatoes, chopped
1 large onion, sliced
1 green pepper, cut into strips
1 red pepper, cut into strips
100 g (approx 3 oz) chicken fillet, cut into strips
1 cup shredded mozzarella cheese
Shredded basil and kaffir lime leaves
Pepper
Olive oil

Pre-heat oven to 200°C. Chop tomatoes roughly. Cut peppers and chicken meat into strips. Slice the onion.

There is no need to thaw out the frozen pizza crust. Just place it on a baking tray and smear green curry paste all over the top. Scatter tomatoes over. Arrange peppers, onions and chicken evenly on the crust. Top with shredded cheese. Using scissors, shred basil and kaffir lime leaves into threads. Scatter over the cheese. Drizzle the lot with a little olive oil.

Cook for 10 minutes or till cheese melts.

TOM YAM KUNG [For 6-8]

4 cups unsalted chicken stock
1-2 tbs bottled tom yam paste
10 prawns, peeled, tails intact
5 straw or abalone mushrooms, cut into half
2 stalks lemon grass, white stem portions, bruised
4 kaffir lime leaves
2 red chillies, cut into two or three
1 tbs fish sauce
Fresh coriander leaves

You could make the stock from scratch in which case you buy a tray of chicken carcasses from the supermarket and boil it up with an onion, a carrot and a stick of celery. If not, just use canned stock.

Bring the stock to boil, then add the bottled paste and the fresh whole herbs - lemon grass, red chillies and kaffir lime leaves. When it comes to the boil, add the prawns and the mushrooms. Taste and season with more fish sauce or a squeeze of lemon if needed. Garnish with coriander leaves.

Our Thai food love affair probably began with this hot sour soup. It suited our tastebuds, already prepped by spicy Malay and Indonesian cuisines. Now it is a standard found in every Thai restaurant in town, and is even cooked in homes, thanks to the bottled seasoning. Here it is made with prawns, though you can substitute prawns with mussels or a selection of seafood. Or you could use chicken pieces instead — in which case, half a cup of coconut milk added to the pot will enrich the flavour.

IKAN BILIS AND PEANUTS [2 jars]

This snack used to be served in bars in the 1950s, before the convenience of packaged cocktail nibbles killed it off.

3 cups ikan bilis (dried anchovies), heads removed
1 cup peanuts, with or without skin
Oil for deep-frying
2 tbs sweet chilli sauce

Rinse dried ikan bilis in running water, then drain and dry with paper towels. Half fill a small wok with oil and heat. Test to see that oil is hot enough by tossing one fish into the oil – it should sizzle.

Fry ikan bilis till brown and crispy. Remove and drain on kitchen paper. Fry peanuts till golden brown. Remove and drain on kitchen paper.

Pour off all but one tablespoon of oil. Replace fried ikan bilis and nuts and drizzle chilli sauce all over. Fry to caramelize and toss to ensure it is well-mixed. Remove and when cool, store in an air-tight jar to ensure that it remains crisp.

BEEF RENDANG [For 6-8]

Rendang was transported to Singapore from Padang, West Sumatra by émigrés with dishes such as sayur lodeh and ayam soto. It is an ideal dish for busy people and with a spice pack on hand, it is a cinch.

1 rendang spice pack
1 kg (2 lb) stewing beef cubes
4 cups coconut milk
1 turmeric leaf, torn into small pieces
4 kaffir lime leaves
1 stalk lemon grass, white stem portion, bruised
2-3 pieces assam gelugor (dried tamarind slices)
1 tsp sugar
1 tsp salt
1 cup grated or dessicated coconut, optional

Place all the ingredients into a large thick-bottomed pot and bring to the boil, then turn down the fire to very low and simmer till liquid has evaporated and beef is tender. Make sure you stir the mixture now and then to ensure that the bottom does not stick. Serve with white rice.

YONG TAUHU WITH SPICY BEAN SAUCE [For 8]

Now that the markets and supermarkets sell readymade yong tauhu – soya bean cakes and vegetables stuffed with fish meat – this popular and healthy hawker dish can be easily replicated at home. Here, a spicy sauce, based again on hoisin sauce, dresses the stuffed items.

A selection of 40-45 pieces of yong taufu
(allow for five or six pieces a head)

Fish stock:
$^1/_2$ cup dried soya beans
$^1/_2$ cup dried ikan bilis (anchovies)
3 cups water

Sauce for one:
1 tbs bottled hoi sin sauce
1 tbs bottled garlic chilli sauce
1 tbs onion oil
    (To make onion oil, zap 2 tbs store-bought fried
    shallots and 1 cup of oil in the microwave oven on
    high for 2-3 minutes.)

Garnish:
Fried shallots
Spring onion, chopped
Pepper
Toasted sesame seeds

Place beans and ikan bilis in a pot large enough for yong taufu items, add water and bring to the boil. Turn down heat and simmer till beans are tender.

Cook the stuffed items in this stock. When they float, they are ready. Remove items with a slotted spoon.

Place the sauce ingredients in a bowl and mix well. Add five or six stuffed items, cut first into bite-sized pieces and toss well.

Garnish with fried shallots, spring onion and a scattering of sesame seeds. Serve with a bowl of clear soup on the side to wash down the meal.

QUICK CHICKEN RICE
[For 6-8]

This Asian bottled sauce, introduced only in the new millennium, is a Godsend for those homesick for Hainanese chicken rice. With more and more Singaporeans working and studying abroad, it conveniently puts together the most essential ingredients of the dish - garlic, ginger, chicken essence and oil - in a bottle.

> 190 g (6 oz) bottle of chicken rice seasoning
> 4 cups of water
> 1 pandan leaf, knotted
> 6 ginger slices
> $1^1/_2$ kg (3 lb) chicken, left whole
> 4 cups of rice
> 4-6 tbs oil (optional)
> 2 stalks spring onions, cut into short lengths
> Bottled chilli garlic sauce
> Black soya sauce

Place the contents of the bottle of chicken rice seasoning and 4 cups of water in a pot. Add a pandan leaf and ginger slices and bring to the boil. Turn down fire to simmer.

Add chicken and cook for 30 minutes over low heat. Allow chicken to cool in the stock. Remove bird and chop into pieces when cooled.

Wash rice and drain. Place rice in a rice cooker, add stock and oil, if using, and cook till grains are dry and fluffy. Serve with chicken pieces, garnished with spring onions, chilli sauce and black soya sauce.

FRIED CHYE TOW KWAY
[For 6-8]

A Chinese breakfast dish that is now eaten at all hours, so popular it is. These days, you need not make the white radish cake (referred to erroneously as carrot cake!) as it is available in slabs on the supermarket shelf. Teochew in origin, it started out fried scrambled, until the 1970s when a smart hawker in Toa Payoh fried it crisp like a pancake, followed soon after by the Hongkong dim sum chef's version - steamed with a seasoned soya sauce. Here is the old-fashioned version.

> 4 radish flour cakes
> 4 tbs vegetable oil or lard
> 1 tbs chopped garlic
> 1 tbs red chilli paste
> 1 tbs chopped chye poh (salted radish)
> 2 eggs
> 1 tbs fish sauce
> 1 stalk fresh spring onion, chopped

Heat two tablespoons of oil or lard in a wok. When smoking hot, brown the radish flour cakes, cutting it into small pieces with the spatula as you fry. Push aside the pieces.

Heat another tablespoon of oil in the wok. Saute garlic and chye poh till browned. Toss with the radish cake pieces. Make a space in the middle, add the last of the oil and break eggs into the space. Leave to set for a few of minutes and then push the radish cake on top.

Drizzle with fish sauce, add chilli paste and toss some more to ensure an even mix. Serve hot garnished with spring onion.

Note: To serve the flour cakes Cantonese style, cut them into four, and steam with seasoned soya sauce made up of $^1/_2$ cup water, 1 tsp sugar, 1 tsp light soya sauce and 2 tbs onion oil (microwave 1 tsp store-bought fried shallots with 2 tbs oil on high for a minute). Garnish with spring onion.

HAR CHEONG KAI [For 6-8]

Introduced to Singapore only in the last 20 years or so, this dish is now a standard at most Cantonese food stalls and at home.

$1^1/_2$ kg (3 lb) chicken, chopped into pieces
Oil for deep-frying

Marinade:
2-3 tbs shrimp sauce
1 tsp sugar
2 tbs rice wine

Make up the marinade and rub it into the chicken pieces. Leave covered in the fridge for three hours, if not overnight.

Fill wok half-full with oil and heat till smoking. Fry chicken pieces till golden brown. Drain on kitchen paper and serve at once with a squeeze of lime juice, if desired. You can also serve the chicken with bottled garlic chilli sauce.

BAK KUT TEH [For 6-8]

1 packet bak kut teh spices
500 g (1 lb) meaty pork ribs
2 whole heads of garlic, unpeeled
1 tbs black soya sauce
6-7 cups of water
1 tbs salt
1-2 heads iceburg lettuce, washed and separated

The spice packet can be used to flavour not only this hearty Hokkien soup, but also any dish that calls for a mix of star anise, cinnamon, cloves, coriander, cumin and fennel. There is also a Teochew version of bak kut teh that is clear and simple, cooked with just garlic, pepper and light soya sauce.

Place ribs, spice packet and garlic in a pot. Add water to cover and bring to the boil. Skim off the meat scum as it rises. Add soya sauce and salt. Reduce heat to simmering and cook till ribs are tender.

Place a few lettuce leaves in the bowl before dishing out the ribs and soup. Serve with white rice and sliced red chillies in dark soya sauce on the side.

CHIRASHI SUSHI
[For 6-8]

Japanese food takes Singapore by storm. This penchant is due not only to increased travel to that country, but also to the large numbers of Japanese living here. In the early 1980s, they formed the biggest expatriate population, leading to the opening of several Japanese restaurants where we all learnt to eat raw fish. And it has become so accepted that today, we can buy all the ingredients for the recipe below at a regular supermarket.

4 cups of short-grain rice
4 cups of water
1 tsp salt
2 tbs rice vinegar
1 tbs sugar

Toppings:
2 tbs marinated seaweed
3-4 slices of smoked salmon, cut into half
2 tbs red salmon eggs
16 slices of a variety of ready sliced sashimi (raw fish)
    or a selection of marinated seafood
Pink Japanese fish floss
1 sheet of nori (toasted seaweed), cut into thin strips
1 Japanese cucumber, sliced
Pickled ginger slices
Wasabi paste
Japanese soya sauce

Wash rice in several changes of water. Place rice in a rice cooker with water and cook till dry and fluffy. When ready, season with salt, vinegar and sugar, mix well and leave uncovered to cool.

When rice is cool, dish out onto a bowl or deep plate. Top with equal proportions of the suggested toppings, except for the dry ingredients such as fish floss and nori, which should be added at the last minute.

Arrange seafood contrasting colours and balancing shapes. Serve at once with cucumber slices, pickled ginger, wasabi and soya sauce on the side.

CHENDOL [For 8-10]

3 cups of chendol strips
300 g (approx 9 oz) gula melaka (palm sugar)
$1^1/_2$ cups water
3 pandan leaves, knotted
4 cups coconut milk
$^1/_4$ tsp salt
Crushed ice

Chop roughly the gula melaka. Place the gula melaka, water and pandan leaves in a heat-proof bowl, and heat in the microwave oven on high for about two minutes. Use a fork to press out any remaining lumps in the syrup. Strain. Add salt to coconut milk and chill in the refrigerator.

To make up drink, place a spoonful of chendol strips into a glass, add ice, sweeten with palm syrup to taste and top up with cold coconut milk.

The chendol strips for this palm-sweetened coconut milk drink are made from green bean flour, coloured with pandan, and pressed through a coarse-holed colander into its characteristic short strips.

A Malay dessert adopted by the nonyas, every South-east Asian country has a version - Indonesia adds giant red beans and Myanmar, sago pearls. In Singapore, we can find red beans, herbal jelly (chin chow) and, these days, even durian puree in the mix.

COCONUT JELLY [Makes a pan]

Coconut milk again flavours this jelly, which became popular when *dim sum* was sold from carts in cavernous dining halls. Today no longer, though it is easy to reproduce this old-fashioned delight with packaged agar-agar (seaweed jelly) powder and coconut milk. In the past, agar agar had to be collected from the beach and dried before making any jelly!

7 g ($^1/_4$ oz) plain agar agar powder (about half a packet)
1 cup water
120 g sugar
1 cup coconut milk
2 pandan leaves, knotted
1 large egg white

Dissolve agar agar in the cup of water and heat. Add sugar and stir till it dissolves. Add pandan leaves and coconut milk and continue heating till it boils. Remove from heat and allow agar mixture to cool slightly. Remove pandan leaves.

While bringing the coconut milk to a boil, whisk egg white till frothy. Fold into agar mixture. Pour into a pan and allow to set in the fridge. Cut into squares and serve cold.

AH BOH LING
IN SOYA BEAN MILK [For 3-4]

Once, ah boh ling was called kway ngee and it came *ko-song* (empty), but in pretty pastel colours. Kway ngee was eaten on the Winter Solstice Festival and other auspicious occasions such as weddings, birthdays and anniversaries as it symbolized unity and harmony. Traditionally the balls would be served simply in clear syrup, though the peranakans would cook it in a delicious rich *pengat* sauce, made from coconut milk and palm sugar.

    1 packet of frozen glutinous rice balls
    500 ml (1 pint) tetrapack of sweetened soya milk

Heat soya milk over a low fire, stirring all the time to prevent curdling till it comes to a simmer. Turn off fire and leave aside.
    Bring a pot of water to boil. Add the frozen balls straight from the packet. Cook till they float. Remove with a slotted spoon and place two or three to a bowl. Ladle over soya milk and serve at once.

BUBUR CHA-CHA [For 8-10]

    4 cups coconut milk
    $1/_2$ cup sugar
    1 cup water
    3 pandan leaves, knotted
    1 packet multi-coloured sago flour cubes
    1 small sweet potato, peeled and cubed
    1 small yam, peeled and cubed

Make syrup by dissolving sugar in a cup of water, together with pandan leaves, in a pot. Add coconut milk and make up to 10 cups of soup by adding more water, if needed. Include the sweet potato and yam cubes, and cook over a low fire till tender. Taste and add more sugar if preferred.
    In another pot, bring some water to the boil and cook the rice flour cubes. When they float, they're ready.
    To serve, place the boiled and drained sago flour cubes, diced yam and sweet potato into a bowl. Pour over the milk and serve hot or cold.

Another traditional coconut milk dessert, this time with sweet potato, yam and colourful chewy flour cubes. Versions of it can be found in the region. Thailand serves what they call red rubies (flour-coated water chestnuts) in coconut milk, and in Singapore now, you can find a jazzed- up version with jackfruit and banana in the bowl.

SOME HERITAGE INGREDIENTS

Bangkwang (Yambean or jicama)
The tuber root of a twining plant. The turnip-shaped root has sand-coloured skin and white crunchy flesh like an unripe pear. Unlike other tubers, it has high water content and has as little as 10 percent starch.

Basmati rice
Basmati means "queen of fragrance". This long-grained, fine-textured rice is valued for its fragrance and nutty flavour.

Belacan (Shrimp paste)
Sold in blocks which range from purplish pink to brownish black, this condiment of salted and dried mashed shrimps is very pungent. It can be found raw in a spice paste for cooking up and is also toasted if used in a dip called sambal chilli.

Buah keras (Candlenuts)
A round, cream-coloured waxy nut. It has an oily consistency and is used to add texture and serve as a thickening agent. Macadamia nuts or raw cashews may be used as substitutes.

Bunga kantan (Pink ginger bud)
This is the flower bud of the Torch Ginger, also known as Phaeomaria. The bud emerges directly from the ground among the leaf stems and opens into a flower like a many-layered lotus blossom.

Chilli padi (bird's eye chilli)
A small chilli, so named because it looks like the eyes of birds. Its size is deceptive because it is one of the most fiery of chillies.

Chinese ham
The origins of Chinese ham or Yunnan ham dates back to the 18th century and comes from the western province of Yunnan. Traditionally made in winter from pork leg, it is smoked or air-dried. This cured ham is deep pink and has a rich, smoky flavour. It can be bought in thick slices or in cans.

Chinese rice wine
Made from fermented glutinous rice or millet, it has a relatively low alcohol content. Aged for ten years or more, the flavourful wine is used both in drinking and cooking. The best wines come from Shaoxing in Zheijang province.

Curry leaves
The leaves of the deciduous curry tree (*Murraya koenigii*) which originates from the Indian subcontinent. The leaflets appear in pairs on a slender stalk. Used fresh or deepfried, it has an unusual scent of curry powder.

Daun kesom (Laksa leaves or Vietnamese mint)
There is no substitute for this herb (*polygonum odoratum*) which has a distinctive lemony smell which some liken to coriander.

Daun limau purut (Kaffir lime leaves)
Has a strong, distinctive fragrance and flavour like a combin-ation of lemongrass and lime. Leaves are about 8 cm long and have two lobes. The plant has long thorns and produce ping-pong ball sized knobbly limes with little juice. The leaves will retain freshness for months if put in the freezer.

Dried scallops
Hard amber disks of dried white scallops, dried scallops are expensive and are used sparingly for flavouring. It can be added to soups and used to enhance gravys, stews, porridge or stir-fries.

Five-spice powder
A blend of anise-pepper, star anise, cassia, cloves and fennel seed.

Ghee
Clarified butter used in traditional Indian cooking. It has a nutty, caramel-like flavour and does not leave a residue.

Gula Melaka (Palm sugar)
Made of juice extracted from the coconut flower. Sold in blocks which are deep honey brown with a caramel taste. Substitute with soft brown sugar.

Hayko (Black prawn paste)
A very thick syrupy paste with a strong shrimp flavour. Not to be confused with belacan (shrimp paste).

Ju her (Cured squid)
This is wet lime-cured squid as opposed to dried squid. Pinkish brown, it is sold whole or cut into pieces.

Kangkong (Water convolvulus)
A member of the morning glory family, this aquatic and semi-aquatic plant has trailing vine-like stems which are hollow so that the plant can float. It has arrow-shaped leaves which are 5-6 inches long.
Kunyit (Tumeric)

Related to ginger, tumeric is pungent and can make food bitter if too much is used. The flesh is a brilliant reddish-orange. It is most commonly available as a powder. It is the poor man's saffron, a substitute to achieve a rich orange colouring in food without the subtle taste.

Lengkwas (Galangal)
Closely resembling ginger, this native of Java is a branched rhizome. It is aromatic, pungent and spicy having been described as both gingery and peppery. Used to flavour soups, stews and curries, it is often pounded with other herbs and spices to make a spice paste.

Lotus seeds
The seeds of the lotus plant which also produces the edible lotus root. The almost-round, cream-coloured seeds are sold dried and has a delicate taste and a slightly powdery texture. Eaten candied or in desserts.

Mok yee (Dried black jelly fungus)
This dark, brown-black fungus is sold dried, looking like small crumpled pieces of black paper. When soaked before use, they swell up into ear shapes. It has no taste of its own but takes on the flavours of other ingredients and is eaten for its slippery texture.

Pandan leaves
The fragrant leaf of a variety of screwpine. It is used for both its colour and fragrance to flavour both desserts and savoury dishes such as coconut rice. Often knotted first before use to release its fragrance.

Pei tan (Century eggs)
Raw duck eggs preserved in lime, ash and salt for up to 100 days. The white turns translucent brown-black and the yolk, creamy and dark greyish blue and green. Has slight fishy taste.

Pomelo
One of the largest citrus fruits, it is slightly pear-shaped. Its thick skin is soft and a thick white membrane covers the flesh which can vary from yellow to tan to pink. Pomelos may be tart to juicy sweet. Select fruits which are sweetly fragrant, heavy for their size and unblemished. Eaten fresh or used in salads, the skin can also be candied.

Sago pearls
Sago is made from a starch extracted from the pithy stem of a mature sago palm. The starch is sieved and then heated to form small pearl-like granules. Popular in desserts.

Serai (Lemon grass)
The plant looks like an untidy clump of tall grass except that it gives off an intensely lemony fragrance. Cut off the roots and peel off the hard outer leaves to use the tender white portion found at the base of the stalk.

Shark's fins
A delicacy in Chinese cuisine. Shark's fin are usually sold dried, either whole, in pieces or in cleaned strands. Frozen prepared fins are also available. The most expensive are those in combs. The fins, prized for their texture, has little flavour of its own and is usually cooked in a rich stock. There is a movement these days to prevent the capture and killing of sharks for just fins.

Tamarind
Bean-shaped dark brown pods of the evergreen tamarind tree. The brittle 5-inch pods conceal a dark pulp which tastes like a combination of apricots, dates and lemons. It is a key ingredient in Worcestershire sauce. Tamarind is used to give chutneys and curries its fruity sourness.

Taucheow (Brown soya bean paste)
A fermented soya bean paste much favoured in Chinese cooking. Some brands have the beans whole while others have the beans mashed.

Taukwa (Firm tofu cakes)
One of many soya products used in Chinese and Southeast Asian cooking. It is made by compressing beancurd to remove most of the water and is sold in squares or larger blocks.

Taupok (Tofu puffs)
Another one of many soya products, this is a deep-fried ball of soya cake which looks like a small brown sponge. Can come in flat squares or in cubes.

Winter melon
This large melon, with its characteristic frosty tint, can weigh up to 30 pounds. Its snowy white porous flesh becomes translucent when cooked.

Water chestnuts
Walnut-sized tuber of a water plant. The skin is brownish-black and when peeled, reveals white, crunchy and juicy flesh.

ABOUT THE AUTHOR

Sylvia Tan is a journalist of long standing whose passion for food has made her one of Singapore's beloved food writers. She is well-known for her down-to-earth approach of making the preparation of delicious food fuss-free.

She wrote the popular "Mad About Food" column in *The Sunday Times* for which she won a special Singapore Press Holdings newspaper award for excellence in 1995. She currently writes a regular column on healthy cooking, "Eat to Live", in T*he Straits Times'* Mind Your Body health supplement and contributes recipes regularly to the Insing food and drink website.

She is the author of eight other books, including: *Mad about Food, Madder Still About Food, Maddest Yet About Food, Homecooked, Modern Nyonya, Asian Larder: Asian Ingredients De-Mystified, Eat to Live* and *Taste: Healthy, Hearty Asian Recipes*, the latter two being compilations of her healthy cooking columns.

ABOUT THE PHOTOGRAPHER

A self taught photographer, Ken Cheong was from 1994 - 2000 a curator of photo collections, Singapore History Museum. He has had two solo photo exhibitions and teaches photography.

The publishers wish to thank the following for their assistance in the publication of this book: Berkeley Restaurant, Kwong Onn Tong, Lau Choy Seng Pte Ltd, Loong Li Chicken and Duck, San Yong Kee Roast Duck and Chicken Rice, Sajis Indian Food Stall and Union Farm Chee Pow Kai.

Additional photographs courtesy of the following,

Ho Keen Fai: pages 40, 44 right, 52 top left and right, 59 both, 60 bottom, 61 top, 72 right, 81 top, 85 bottom, 92 bottom left and top right, 102 bottom, 104, 105 top right, 106 top, 109 bottom, 112 right, 113, 115 both, 122 bottom, 125 top right, 127 top.

National Archives of Singapore: pages 4 left, 7 left, 8 both, 9 left, 10, 12 bottom left, 19 bottom right, 22 centre left, 28, 33 bottom right, 41 bottom left, 50, 52 bottom left and right, 65 top, 66 bottom, 70, 72 bottom left, 76 bottom, 77 top, 95 bottom, 96, 107 bottom.

Singapore Cold Storage: pages 2 right, 6 right, 7 right, 12 top right, 18, 21 top right, 27 bottom, 30, 33 top left, 49 bottom right, 126 bottom.

Tan Ngiap Heng: page 32, top right

Revised edition 2014

Text © Sylvia Tan, 2004
Food photographs © Ken Cheong, 2004

Published by
Landmark Books Pte Ltd
5001, Beach Road, #02-73/74,
Singapore 199588

978-981-4189-50-7

Also published as *The Cold Storage Heritage Food Cookbook*.

Printed in Singapore